The Ultimate Mortgage Payoff Game Plan

How to Combine Multiple Mortgage Strategies into a Step-by-Step Plan for Financial Freedom

By Joseph G. Correa

Copyright & Legal Notice

Published by Live Stronger Faster

First Edition, 2026

Table of Contents

Introduction

For many people, a mortgage is the single largest financial obligation they will ever carry. It can follow them for decades, shape their monthly budget, influence their career choices, delay retirement, and create stress that quietly affects every aspect of life. Yet despite the emotional and financial weight attached to a mortgage, most homeowners never receive a true education on how to strategically manage it. They are taught how to qualify for a loan, how to make a monthly payment, and how to avoid default, but they are rarely taught how to build a long-term mortgage elimination plan that aligns with wealth creation, financial freedom, and personal goals. That is exactly why this book exists.

Throughout this series, you have explored a wide range of mortgage payoff strategies. You learned how to accelerate principal reduction without sacrificing your quality of life. You discovered how biweekly payment structures can quietly shave years off a loan term. You explored the power of lump-sum reductions, refinancing strategies, rental income, house hacking, and cash-flow optimization. You also examined more advanced concepts such as strategic leverage, real estate investing while paying off debt, and the use of income acceleration systems to build wealth faster. Individually, each strategy can be powerful. However, the true transformation happens when these strategies are combined into a personalized and intentional mortgage payoff blueprint.

That is the focus of this final book in the series.

This book is not about one isolated tactic or one universal solution. Instead, it is about integration. It is about understanding how different financial tools, income sources, debt reduction methods, and investment strategies can work together as part of a complete financial game plan. The ultimate mortgage payoff strategy is not simply making larger payments every month. It is building a coordinated system that improves cash flow, increases flexibility, reduces financial stress, and accelerates wealth creation simultaneously.

One of the biggest mistakes homeowners make is assuming there is only one "correct" way to eliminate a mortgage. Some people aggressively pay off their loan as quickly as possible regardless of opportunity cost. Others endlessly refinance or leverage equity without a clear long-term strategy. Some focus exclusively on investing and ignore debt management completely. The truth is that financial success rarely comes from extremes. Instead, sustainable wealth is often created through balance, adaptability, and intelligent decision-making based on personal circumstances. A mortgage payoff game plan should evolve as your life evolves.

Your income may increase. Your family situation may change. Interest rates may rise or fall. Investment opportunities may appear. You may transition from employee income to business ownership or from active income to passive income. Your priorities at age thirty may be dramatically different from your priorities at age fifty-five. Because of this, a rigid one-size-fits-all strategy rarely works over the long term. The most successful homeowners learn how to adapt their mortgage strategy to changing financial conditions while staying focused on the larger goal of financial freedom.

Financial freedom means different things to different people. For some, it means eliminating monthly debt obligations completely and living with peace of mind. For others, it means creating enough investment income to comfortably cover housing expenses. Some people want to retire early without a mortgage payment. Others want to use their home strategically while building a portfolio of rental properties or businesses. Regardless of the exact vision, one principle remains constant: controlling your mortgage instead of allowing your mortgage to control you is one of the most powerful financial shifts you can make.

This book is designed to help you create that shift.

One important idea you will encounter throughout this book is that financial acceleration is often more about systems than sacrifice. Many homeowners believe the only way to pay off a mortgage early is through extreme budgeting, deprivation, or working endless hours. While discipline certainly matters, long-term financial success becomes far more sustainable when systems are designed intelligently. Improving cash flow, reducing unnecessary interest expense, increasing income efficiency, using tax advantages wisely, and redirecting money strategically can often create dramatic progress without destroying lifestyle or motivation.

This is especially important in today's economic environment. Rising living costs, inflation, fluctuating interest rates, and economic uncertainty have created financial pressure for millions of households. Many homeowners feel trapped between wanting to build wealth and needing to maintain stability. Some worry about retirement savings while still carrying decades of mortgage debt ahead of them. Others feel frustrated because despite earning a good income, they do not feel financially free. This book addresses those concerns by focusing not only on debt reduction, but also on long-term wealth optimization.

Another critical lesson you will learn is that mortgage payoff should never happen in isolation from the rest of your financial life. Too often, homeowners focus exclusively on eliminating debt while neglecting emergency reserves, retirement planning, investment opportunities, business growth, or income development. In some situations, aggressively paying off a mortgage may be the smartest move available. In other cases, balancing mortgage reduction with strategic investing may create greater long-term results. The key is understanding how to evaluate trade-offs intelligently rather than emotionally.

Emotions play a powerful role in mortgage decisions.

Fear, stress, pride, impatience, and even social pressure can influence financial choices more than logic. Some people rush to eliminate debt because they crave emotional security. Others avoid paying down debt because they fear missing investment opportunities. Some refinance repeatedly without a clear objective simply because it temporarily lowers monthly payments. Financial clarity comes from understanding not only the mathematics behind mortgage acceleration, but also the psychology behind financial decision-making.

This book will help you think strategically rather than react emotionally.

You will learn how to evaluate your current financial position honestly and build a realistic roadmap based on your goals, risk tolerance, income structure, and stage of life. You will explore how to combine income growth strategies with debt reduction strategies. You will learn how to prioritize cash flow management, liquidity, and long-term flexibility while still aggressively moving toward mortgage freedom. Most importantly, you will learn how to create a repeatable financial framework that can continue working for you long after your mortgage is gone.

The journey toward mortgage freedom is not only financial. It is personal.

For many people, eliminating a mortgage represents freedom from stress, freedom from dependency, and freedom from financial limitation. It can provide peace of mind during economic downturns, increase retirement flexibility, and create greater opportunities for family stability and generational wealth. A paid-off home can reduce monthly obligations dramatically and allow income to be redirected toward investments, travel, charitable giving, entrepreneurship, or lifestyle improvement.

At the same time, this book will encourage you to think beyond the simple idea of "debt-free." True wealth is not just about eliminating obligations. It is about creating options. Financial strength comes from having flexibility, control, liquidity, confidence, and the ability to make life decisions without constant financial pressure. Sometimes that includes aggressively paying down debt. Sometimes it includes strategically using leverage to create greater long-term opportunities. The ultimate goal is not merely mortgage elimination. The ultimate goal is financial empowerment.

You will also discover that consistency matters more than perfection. Many homeowners become discouraged because they believe financial success requires perfect timing, flawless investing, or massive income. In reality, long-term financial freedom is usually built through steady progress, intelligent habits, and disciplined decision-making repeated consistently over time. Small adjustments in spending, saving, investing, and debt management can compound into extraordinary results over years and decades.

This book is intended to serve as both a strategic guide and a long-term financial blueprint. It brings together the principles explored throughout the series and organizes them into a practical and adaptable framework. Whether you are just beginning your mortgage payoff journey or already implementing advanced wealth-building strategies, the lessons in this book can help you create a more intentional path forward.

By the end of this book, you will understand how to:

- Build a personalized mortgage payoff roadmap based on your financial goals
- Combine multiple payoff methods for maximum efficiency
- Improve cash flow while accelerating debt reduction
- Balance mortgage payoff with investing and wealth creation
- Use refinancing, income growth, and real estate strategically
- Avoid common financial mistakes that slow progress
- Create long-term financial security and flexibility
- Design a sustainable system that supports both freedom and growth

Most importantly, you will learn that financial freedom is not reserved for the wealthy, the lucky, or the financially gifted. It is available to individuals who are willing to think strategically, stay disciplined, and consistently move forward with purpose.

Your mortgage does not have to define your future. With the right strategy, the right mindset, and the right long-term plan, your mortgage can become a stepping stone rather than a limitation. It can become part of a larger system that supports wealth creation, financial confidence, and long-term freedom for you and your family.

This book is your roadmap for building that future.

Chapter 1

Building Your Ultimate Mortgage Payoff Blueprint

Most homeowners begin their mortgage journey with one primary goal: getting approved for the loan. They spend weeks gathering documents, reviewing credit, verifying income, comparing interest rates, and signing paperwork. Once the loan closes, many people feel a sense of relief and accomplishment because they finally own a home. However, what most borrowers fail to realize is that the closing table is not the finish line. It is the beginning of a long-term financial journey that can either create stress and financial pressure or become one of the greatest wealth-building opportunities of their lives.

The difference between these two outcomes is rarely determined by income alone. It is usually determined by strategy.

Many people with high incomes remain trapped in debt for decades because they lack a clear financial system. At the same time, some moderate-income households achieve extraordinary financial freedom because they create intentional plans that align spending, investing, debt reduction, and cash flow management together. The purpose of this chapter is to help you begin building your own mortgage payoff blueprint—a personalized financial framework designed to help you reduce debt faster, improve cash flow, increase flexibility, and create long-term wealth.

The first step in creating an effective mortgage payoff blueprint is understanding your current financial position honestly. Many homeowners avoid fully analyzing their finances because they fear what they might discover. They know their mortgage payment, but they may not know how much interest they will pay over the life of the loan. They may not understand how much of each payment actually goes toward principal reduction in the early years of the mortgage. Some borrowers are surprised to discover that during the first several years of a traditional thirty-year mortgage, a very large percentage of each monthly payment goes toward interest instead of ownership equity.

Understanding this reality can completely change your perspective on debt.

For example, a homeowner with a large mortgage balance and a moderate interest rate could end up paying hundreds of thousands of dollars in interest over the life of the loan. Many people accept this as normal simply because they were never taught that alternative strategies exist. However, once homeowners understand how amortization works and how interest compounds over time, they often become motivated to seek more efficient ways to manage debt and accelerate financial freedom.

One of the most important concepts in mortgage acceleration is realizing that time matters just as much as payment size. Small extra principal payments made early in the loan term can often create dramatic long-term savings because they reduce the balance that future interest calculations are based upon. This means that strategic timing can significantly improve financial efficiency even when the extra payment amounts are relatively modest.

However, an effective mortgage payoff blueprint is not simply about sending random extra payments whenever possible. It requires organization, consistency, and alignment with larger financial goals. Before aggressively paying down a mortgage, homeowners should evaluate their complete financial situation, including emergency savings, consumer debt, retirement accounts, investment opportunities, income stability, and future plans.

For example, someone with high-interest credit card debt may benefit more from eliminating that debt first before aggressively attacking a low-interest mortgage. Another person with unstable income may prioritize building larger emergency reserves before accelerating mortgage payments. A business owner may choose to maintain liquidity for investment opportunities while still gradually reducing mortgage debt. The key is understanding that mortgage payoff should work together with your overall financial life instead of competing against it.

Creating a blueprint requires clarity.

Clarity begins with defining your financial goals. Some homeowners want to eliminate their mortgage before retirement. Others want to reduce financial stress and monthly obligations as quickly as possible. Some individuals are focused on maximizing investment growth while maintaining manageable mortgage debt. Others want to create generational wealth through real estate ownership and passive income. Your mortgage strategy should reflect your personal vision rather than someone else's definition of success.

One of the most powerful exercises you can do is calculate what your financial life would look like without a mortgage payment. Imagine redirecting thousands of dollars each month toward investments, travel, family goals, charitable causes, or business opportunities. Imagine entering retirement without a large monthly housing expense. Imagine the emotional relief of knowing your home is fully paid for regardless of economic conditions. These possibilities are not fantasies reserved for the wealthy. They become realistic outcomes when financial decisions are made intentionally over time.

At the same time, it is important to recognize that paying off a mortgage early is not always the only objective. Financial flexibility also matters. Some homeowners become so obsessed with eliminating debt that they sacrifice liquidity and place themselves in vulnerable positions. A strong mortgage payoff blueprint balances aggression with stability. It creates progress while protecting financial security.

This balance becomes especially important during economic uncertainty. Life is unpredictable. Job changes, medical expenses, recessions, market volatility, and family emergencies can occur unexpectedly. Homeowners who maintain healthy cash reserves and financial flexibility are often better positioned to navigate these challenges without panic. This is why a mortgage payoff strategy should include emergency planning as part of the blueprint.

Income growth also plays a major role in accelerating mortgage freedom. Many people focus entirely on reducing expenses, but increasing income can sometimes create even greater financial acceleration. Side businesses, investment income, rental income, commissions, freelance work, digital products, and career advancement can all provide additional cash flow that may be strategically directed toward debt reduction and wealth creation.

One of the most effective ways to accelerate mortgage payoff without sacrificing lifestyle is learning how to redirect new income streams rather than relying solely on cutting existing expenses. For example, a homeowner may choose to allocate bonuses, raises, rental profits, or side income specifically toward mortgage principal reduction. Because this money was not previously part of the household budget, the strategy often feels less restrictive while still creating significant financial progress.

Your blueprint should also include clear systems for managing spending behavior. Financial success is rarely destroyed by one catastrophic decision. More often, it is gradually weakened by small, repeated habits that create long-term inefficiency. Lifestyle inflation is one of the greatest threats to financial acceleration. As income rises, many people automatically increase spending on cars, entertainment, vacations, subscriptions, and luxury purchases. While enjoying life is important, uncontrolled lifestyle expansion can delay financial freedom by years or even decades. This does not mean you must live an extreme or deprived lifestyle. The goal is intentionality. Every dollar should have a purpose. Some dollars are directed toward present enjoyment. Others are directed toward future freedom. A successful mortgage payoff blueprint creates a balance between living well today and building security for tomorrow.

Another critical element of the blueprint is understanding the role of interest rates. Interest rates influence not only monthly payments but also long-term opportunity costs. In certain situations, refinancing may dramatically improve financial efficiency by reducing interest expense or shortening loan terms. In other cases, homeowners may intentionally maintain low-interest debt while directing excess cash toward higher-return investment opportunities.

There is no universal answer that applies to every homeowner. Financial strategy depends on timing, goals, risk tolerance, income stability, and market conditions. This is why personalized planning is so important. The best financial decisions are often based on long-term thinking rather than emotional reactions to headlines or market trends.

As you continue building your mortgage payoff blueprint, it is important to remember that wealth creation is a process. Many people become discouraged because they expect instant transformation. However, financial freedom is usually built gradually through consistent progress. Every extra payment, every intelligent decision, every avoided mistake, and every strategic investment contributes to long-term momentum.

Momentum is powerful.

Once homeowners begin seeing progress, they often become more motivated and disciplined. Watching a mortgage balance decrease faster than expected can create excitement and confidence. Increased equity can provide flexibility and opportunities. Reduced debt obligations can improve peace of mind. Over time, these improvements compound into greater financial control and personal freedom.

Technology and automation can also strengthen your blueprint. Automatic transfers, scheduled principal payments, investment contributions, budgeting software, and cash-flow tracking systems can reduce decision fatigue and increase consistency. Financial systems work best when they become habits rather than occasional acts of motivation.

This chapter is not about creating perfection. It is about creating direction.

Your blueprint does not need to be flawless from the beginning. It simply needs to provide a structured path forward. You can refine your strategy over time as your income, goals, and life circumstances evolve. What matters most is developing awareness, discipline, and intentionality.

The homeowners who achieve long-term financial freedom are usually not the ones who make the most money. They are often the individuals who consistently align their financial decisions with their larger goals. They understand the difference between temporary satisfaction and lasting freedom. They learn how to manage cash flow wisely, reduce unnecessary interest costs, increase income opportunities, and maintain focus during difficult periods.

Most importantly, they take action.

A mortgage payoff blueprint is valuable only if it is implemented. Knowledge without action creates no results. The strategies in this series are designed to empower you with options, but ultimately your future will be shaped by the financial habits and decisions you practice consistently over time.

Your mortgage does not have to remain a thirty-year burden.

With discipline, strategy, and long-term thinking, it can become a temporary phase that leads to financial independence, wealth creation, and a more secure future. The process begins with building a blueprint that reflects your personal goals, your financial reality, and your long-term vision for freedom.

This chapter is the foundation of that blueprint. The chapters that follow will help you strengthen, refine, and accelerate the plan until financial freedom becomes not just a possibility, but a realistic and achievable outcome.

The Family That Refused to Stay Financially Stuck

Michael and Elena Ramirez sat quietly at their kitchen table long after their children had gone to bed. The house was finally silent except for the low hum of the refrigerator and the distant sound of rain outside. A stack of unopened bills sat in the center of the table beside Michael's laptop, and Elena stared at the mortgage statement with frustration written across her face.

"We've been paying this mortgage for almost eight years," she said softly. "And somehow it still feels like we barely own the house."

Michael leaned back in his chair and rubbed his forehead. He had worked overtime nearly every weekend for the past six months at the logistics company where he managed warehouse operations, yet their financial progress felt painfully slow.

Between the mortgage, property taxes, groceries, car payments, insurance, and childcare expenses, every month felt like a race they could barely finish. "We make more money now than we ever did before," Michael said. "But it still feels like we're stuck."

Elena nodded. That feeling haunted both of them.

Years earlier, buying their home had represented success. They remembered the excitement of getting approved for the mortgage, touring the property with their realtor, and imagining family dinners, birthday parties, and holiday celebrations in the house. At the time, the monthly payment seemed manageable. But over the years, life became more expensive. Their income increased, but so did their obligations.

What frustrated Elena most was the realization that despite years of payments, the loan balance still felt enormous. Earlier that evening she had searched online for a mortgage amortization calculator and discovered how much interest they would pay over the full thirty-year term if they continued making only minimum payments.

The number shocked her.

"We're giving the bank hundreds of thousands of dollars," she whispered.

Michael stared silently at the statement.

For the first time, they both realized something important: they had spent years working hard without an actual financial strategy. They had goals, dreams, and good intentions, but no organized system guiding their decisions.

That night became a turning point.

Instead of feeling defeated, they decided to get honest about their finances. They listed every monthly expense, every debt, every source of income, and every financial goal. The process was uncomfortable at first. They discovered small spending habits that added up to large amounts over time. Multiple subscriptions, restaurant meals, impulse purchases, and unnecessary expenses had quietly drained their cash flow month after month.

But they also discovered something encouraging.

They were not hopeless.

In fact, they realized they had more financial potential than they originally believed.

Elena began researching mortgage payoff strategies and financial planning concepts late at night after the children went to sleep. She learned about principal reduction, refinancing options, cash-flow optimization, and investment strategies. Michael started listening to financial audiobooks during his commute to work. Slowly, they began changing the way they thought about money.

Instead of reacting emotionally to financial stress, they started building systems.

The first change they made was simple. They created automatic extra principal payments every month, even if the amount was relatively small. They also redirected Michael's overtime income entirely toward debt reduction instead of allowing it to disappear into miscellaneous spending.

Three months later, Elena started a small online bookkeeping service for local business owners. The extra income was modest initially, but instead of increasing their lifestyle, they applied most of it toward debt reduction and emergency savings.

For the first time in years, they began feeling momentum.

They watched their mortgage balance decrease faster than expected. Their emergency fund grew steadily. Small financial wins began replacing the stress and hopelessness they once felt.

Then something unexpected happened.

Michael received a promotion opportunity at work, but it required additional training certifications. Years earlier, they would have hesitated because of the cost. But because they had improved their financial organization and cash reserves, they felt confident investing in his career advancement. Within a year, Michael's income increased significantly.

Instead of immediately upgrading cars or increasing lifestyle spending, they stayed disciplined. They refinanced their mortgage into a shorter term with a better interest rate while maintaining manageable monthly payments. Elena's bookkeeping business also continued growing through referrals.

By the third year of their financial transformation, they had paid off all consumer debt except the mortgage. More importantly, they no longer felt trapped financially. They had options.

The emotional change inside the family was just as significant as the financial improvement.

Michael slept better at night. Elena felt less anxious about unexpected expenses. Family conversations shifted from stress and worry toward future goals and opportunities. They started talking about investments, travel, and eventually helping their children avoid the financial mistakes they themselves had made earlier in life.

One evening, Michael sat outside on the back patio watching his son practice baseball swings in the yard. Elena walked outside carrying two cups of coffee.

"You know what's strange?" Michael said.

"What?"

"I used to think financial freedom meant becoming rich overnight. Now I realize it's really about control."

Elena smiled because she understood exactly what he meant.

Control meant no longer panicking over unexpected bills. It meant having savings. It meant understanding where their money was going. It meant making decisions intentionally instead of emotionally. It meant knowing their future was improving because of the systems they had built together.

Five years after that difficult night at the kitchen table, their lives looked completely different.

Their mortgage balance had been reduced dramatically ahead of schedule. Elena's business generated reliable recurring income. Michael had advanced further in his career than he ever expected. They owned a small rental property producing additional monthly cash flow. Most importantly, they no longer felt financially trapped.

Friends and family often asked them what changed.

Some assumed they must have inherited money or experienced sudden success. But Michael and Elena always gave the same answer.

"We stopped living without a plan."

Their transformation had not come from luck. It came from awareness, discipline, consistency, and strategy repeated over time.

The greatest lesson they learned was that financial freedom is rarely created through one giant breakthrough. More often, it is built through hundreds of intelligent decisions made consistently over many years. Small actions compound. Systems compound. Habits compound.

And eventually, those small changes create an entirely different life.

Years later, after making their final mortgage payment, Michael and Elena sat together once again at the same kitchen table where their transformation had begun. But this time there were no piles of bills, no fear, and no frustration.

Only peace.

Elena looked around the house and smiled quietly.

"This home finally belongs to us," she said.

Michael nodded. But deep down, they both understood something even more important. The real victory was not simply paying off the house.

The real victory was becoming the type of people capable of building lasting financial freedom together.

Chapter 2

Understanding Cash Flow: The Foundation of Mortgage Freedom

One of the greatest financial misunderstandings among homeowners is the belief that income alone determines financial success. Many people assume that individuals with large salaries automatically achieve financial freedom faster than everyone else. While income certainly matters, the reality is that countless high earners remain trapped in debt for decades because they fail to control and direct their cash flow effectively. At the same time, many moderate-income households quietly build substantial wealth because they understand how to manage money strategically. The difference often comes down to one critical concept: cash flow.

Cash flow is the movement of money into and out of your financial life. It is not simply about how much money you make. It is about how efficiently you manage, protect, direct, and multiply the money that passes through your hands every month. Homeowners who master cash flow gain one of the most powerful advantages in the journey toward mortgage freedom and long-term wealth creation. A mortgage is deeply connected to cash flow because it is typically the largest recurring monthly expense most households carry. When a significant percentage of monthly income is consumed by housing costs, it limits flexibility, slows wealth-building opportunities, and increases financial stress. However, homeowners who improve their cash flow position can accelerate principal reduction, increase savings, invest strategically, and create greater financial stability without necessarily needing massive income increases.

Understanding cash flow begins with awareness.

Most people know approximately how much money they earn each month, but far fewer understand exactly where their money goes. Small spending habits often escape attention because they feel insignificant individually. Coffee purchases, delivery services, subscriptions, dining out, impulse shopping, convenience spending, and entertainment costs may seem harmless in isolation, but over time they can quietly consume thousands of dollars that could have been directed toward debt reduction or investment growth.

This does not mean that every enjoyable expense should be eliminated. Financial freedom is not about punishment. It is about intentionality. The goal is not to remove all pleasure from life. The goal is to ensure that spending aligns with priorities and long-term goals.

One of the most effective exercises homeowners can perform is conducting a complete cash-flow audit. This process involves reviewing every recurring expense, every debt obligation, and every source of income honestly. Many people are surprised when they see how much money leaks out of their finances through habits that provide little long-term value.

For example, a household may discover that small recurring subscriptions add up to several hundred dollars per month. Dining expenses may exceed expectations. High-interest debt payments may be consuming enormous amounts of cash flow that could otherwise be building equity or investments. Once these patterns become visible, homeowners gain the power to make intentional adjustments.

A cash-flow audit is not about guilt. It is about clarity.

Clarity creates control. Control creates options.

When homeowners improve cash flow, even modestly, the impact can become significant over time. An extra few hundred dollars per month directed toward mortgage principal reduction can shorten a loan term dramatically while reducing long-term interest costs. Likewise, improved cash flow can strengthen emergency savings, reduce reliance on credit cards, and create opportunities for investment growth.

One important principle in cash-flow management is understanding the difference between productive and unproductive debt. Not all debt is equal. High-interest consumer debt, such as credit cards with large balances, often destroys cash flow because interest payments consume income without creating long-term value. Mortgage debt, while still an obligation, may be tied to an appreciating asset and may offer tax advantages or long-term equity growth.

This distinction matters because homeowners must prioritize financial decisions strategically. Someone carrying high-interest credit card debt while aggressively prepaying a low-interest mortgage may unintentionally slow overall financial progress. In many situations, eliminating high-interest obligations first can free up substantial monthly cash flow that can later be redirected toward mortgage acceleration.

Cash flow is also heavily influenced by lifestyle inflation.

Lifestyle inflation occurs when spending increases automatically alongside income increases. A raise at work leads to a larger car payment. A successful business year leads to luxury purchases. Increased income creates larger monthly obligations instead of greater financial freedom. Over time, people earning excellent incomes may still feel financially trapped because their expenses expanded as quickly as their earnings.

This cycle is extremely common.

Many homeowners believe they will finally feel financially comfortable once they reach a certain income level, only to discover that higher earnings alone do not solve poor cash-flow habits. Without intentional planning, spending simply adjusts upward.

The most financially successful individuals often follow a different pattern. Instead of immediately increasing lifestyle spending every time income rises, they strategically allocate portions of new income toward debt reduction, investing, savings, or income-producing assets. This creates financial acceleration rather than financial stagnation.

Mortgage freedom becomes far more achievable when income growth is paired with disciplined cash-flow management.

Another powerful aspect of cash-flow optimization is increasing income efficiency. Many homeowners focus exclusively on reducing expenses while ignoring income opportunities that may dramatically improve financial flexibility. Side businesses, freelance work, rental income, digital products, commissions, consulting, and investments can all increase cash flow significantly over time.

In today's economy, multiple income streams are becoming increasingly important. Relying entirely on one paycheck can create vulnerability, especially during economic uncertainty. Additional income streams not only improve financial stability but also accelerate mortgage reduction without forcing extreme lifestyle sacrifices.

For example, a homeowner who creates an additional $1,000 per month in side income and consistently applies that money toward mortgage principal may save tens or even hundreds of thousands of dollars in interest over the life of the loan. More importantly, the psychological effect of accelerating progress often increases motivation and financial discipline.

Cash flow also affects emotional well-being.

Financial stress is one of the leading sources of anxiety in modern life. When homeowners constantly feel pressured by bills and debt obligations, it can affect sleep, relationships, career decisions, and overall quality of life. Improved cash flow creates breathing room. It provides flexibility during emergencies and reduces dependence on credit during difficult periods.

This emotional component of financial freedom is often underestimated.

A homeowner with strong cash reserves, manageable expenses, and improving mortgage equity may feel significantly more secure than someone earning twice as much but living paycheck to paycheck under overwhelming financial pressure. True financial strength comes not only from income but from stability, control, and flexibility.

Technology can also play a major role in improving cash-flow management. Automated budgeting systems, spending trackers, investment apps, automatic transfers, and debt payoff calculators can simplify financial organization and reduce emotional decision-making. Automation helps transform good intentions into consistent habits.

For example, automatically directing extra funds toward principal reduction immediately after payday prevents money from being spent impulsively elsewhere. Automated savings contributions strengthen emergency reserves without requiring constant willpower. These systems create momentum while reducing mental stress.

Another critical factor in cash-flow management is preparing for irregular expenses. Many households struggle financially not because they lack income, but because they fail to anticipate predictable expenses. Car repairs, insurance renewals, holidays, property taxes, school expenses, and medical bills often create financial panic because no system was established to prepare for them.

A strong mortgage payoff plan includes preparation.

Setting aside funds gradually for future expenses improves stability and prevents reliance on credit cards or emergency borrowing. This preserves cash flow and protects long-term financial progress.

It is also important to recognize that cash flow changes throughout life. Younger homeowners may prioritize income growth and debt reduction aggressively. Families with children may experience higher monthly obligations temporarily. Older homeowners approaching retirement may shift focus toward debt elimination and income preservation. Financial strategies should evolve with life stages.

Flexibility is essential.

Rigid financial systems often fail because life itself is unpredictable. The goal is not perfection. The goal is adaptability combined with consistent forward movement.

One of the greatest advantages of improving cash flow is that it creates options. Homeowners with strong cash flow can refinance strategically, invest during opportunities, survive economic downturns more comfortably, and make long-term decisions with greater confidence. Options reduce stress and increase freedom. As homeowners gain control over cash flow, they often experience a mindset shift. Instead of feeling controlled by bills and obligations, they begin viewing money as a tool for creating opportunities and building stability. This transformation changes financial behavior dramatically.

Mortgage freedom is not achieved through random luck.

It is built through awareness, intentionality, discipline, and systems repeated consistently over time. Cash flow serves as the engine powering that entire process. Without strong cash-flow management, even large incomes can disappear quickly. With strong cash-flow management, financial progress becomes sustainable and measurable.

This chapter is intended to help you recognize that mortgage acceleration is not only about making extra payments. It is about strengthening the entire financial structure supporting those payments. A homeowner with strong cash flow gains the ability to move faster, recover from setbacks more effectively, and create long-term wealth with greater confidence.

Your mortgage payoff blueprint depends on cash flow because cash flow determines flexibility, stability, and opportunity.

The stronger your cash flow becomes, the stronger your financial future becomes.

The Couple Who Learned That More Income Wasn't the Answer

Daniel and Sophia Carter believed they were doing everything right.

They had good jobs, a beautiful home in a growing neighborhood, two reliable vehicles, and enough income to live what most people would consider a comfortable life. Daniel worked as a regional sales manager for a technology company, while Sophia managed marketing operations for a healthcare firm. Combined, they earned more money than either of their parents had ever made.

Yet every month felt stressful.

No matter how much they earned, there never seemed to be enough left over.

One Friday evening, Daniel walked through the front door after a long week of work and immediately sensed Sophia's frustration. She sat at the kitchen counter staring silently at her laptop.

"What happened?" he asked carefully.

Sophia turned the screen toward him.

Their checking account balance was far lower than expected.

Again.

Daniel sighed heavily. "I don't understand how this keeps happening."

Neither did Sophia.

They paid their bills on time. They earned strong incomes. They rarely considered themselves irresponsible. Yet somehow they constantly felt financially stretched. Credit card balances slowly increased despite monthly payments. Their savings account barely grew. Unexpected expenses created panic instead of inconvenience.

The mortgage payment alone consumed a huge portion of their monthly income, but it was not the only issue. Car payments, subscriptions, restaurant spending, travel, online shopping, and rising living costs quietly drained their finances month after month.

The frustrating part was that they truly believed they were financially successful.

From the outside, they looked successful.

Inside, they felt trapped.

One evening, after another stressful conversation about money, Sophia suggested something uncomfortable.

"I think we need to actually look at everything," she said.

Daniel resisted at first. Like many people, he preferred avoiding detailed financial analysis because it created anxiety. But eventually he agreed.

The following Saturday morning, they sat together at the dining room table with printed bank statements, credit card statements, and budgeting worksheets spread across the surface.

The numbers shocked them.

Individually, most of their expenses seemed harmless. A streaming service here. Restaurant dinners there. Frequent coffee stops. Weekend shopping trips. Subscription apps they barely used. Convenience purchases. Delivery fees. Small impulse spending throughout the month.

But together, the total was staggering.

They realized they were leaking enormous amounts of money without intention.

More importantly, they discovered something even bigger: every time their income increased over the years, their lifestyle increased with it. Raises had not created financial freedom. They had simply created larger obligations.

Daniel leaned back in his chair and stared at the spreadsheet silently.

"We make too much money to feel this broke," he said.

Sophia nodded slowly.

For the first time, they understood the real problem was not income. It was cash flow management.

That realization changed everything.

Instead of focusing only on earning more money, they began redesigning their financial system. They canceled subscriptions they did not truly value. They reduced unnecessary spending gradually without making life miserable. They created automatic savings transfers and scheduled extra mortgage principal payments immediately after payday.

Most importantly, they gave every dollar a purpose.

At first, the changes felt uncomfortable. Habits were difficult to break. Daniel especially struggled with impulse spending because he often used purchases as a reward after stressful workweeks.

But slowly, progress became visible. Their savings account started growing consistently. Credit card balances began shrinking. The stress surrounding money conversations decreased significantly.

Then Sophia made another suggestion.

"What if we created another income stream instead of just cutting expenses?"

The idea stayed in Daniel's mind for weeks.

Eventually, he began consulting small businesses on sales systems during evenings and weekends. The extra income started slowly, but within several months it became substantial. Instead of spending the money, they directed almost all of it toward debt reduction and investments.

For the first time in years, they felt momentum instead of pressure.

Two years later, their financial situation looked dramatically different.

Their emergency fund was fully established. Their consumer debt was nearly gone. Their mortgage balance was decreasing much faster than scheduled. Daniel's consulting business had grown into a reliable secondary income source, and Sophia had negotiated flexible remote work arrangements that improved both income stability and lifestyle balance.

But the biggest transformation was emotional.

Money no longer controlled their relationship.

Before improving their cash flow systems, financial stress constantly created tension between them. Small purchases triggered arguments. Unexpected expenses caused panic. Conversations about the future felt uncertain and frustrating.

Now, they felt aligned.

One evening, while reviewing their updated mortgage payoff projections, Sophia smiled as she pointed at the screen.

"If we stay consistent, we could pay this house off years earlier than we originally planned."

Daniel stared at the numbers quietly.

Years earlier, the idea would have seemed impossible.

Now it felt inevitable.

"What's strange," Daniel said thoughtfully, "is that I used to think financial freedom meant making more money."

Sophia smiled.

"And now?" He looked around the kitchen—the same room where they once felt overwhelmed by bills and stress.

"Now I think it means controlling where the money goes."

That realization became the foundation of their new financial life.

Over the following years, they continued strengthening their cash flow systems. Instead of reacting emotionally to money, they made intentional decisions aligned with long-term goals. They increased investments gradually, accelerated mortgage payments strategically, and maintained financial flexibility instead of allowing lifestyle inflation to take control again.

By their early fifties, they had achieved something neither thought possible years earlier.

Their mortgage was nearly eliminated.

More importantly, they no longer feared the future financially.

They had learned one of the most important lessons in wealth creation: financial freedom is not built by income alone. It is built by mastering cash flow, creating intentional systems, and consistently directing money toward long-term priorities instead of short-term emotional spending.

And once they understood that lesson, everything about their future changed.

Chapter 3

Creating a Personalized Mortgage Acceleration Strategy

One of the most common financial mistakes homeowners make is attempting to follow someone else's mortgage payoff plan without considering their own financial reality, lifestyle, goals, and risk tolerance. A strategy that works perfectly for one household may create unnecessary stress or even financial instability for another. This is why creating a personalized mortgage acceleration strategy is so important. Financial freedom is not built through imitation alone. It is built through alignment between your financial decisions and your unique circumstances.

A mortgage acceleration strategy is more than simply paying extra toward principal every month. It is a coordinated system designed to reduce debt efficiently while maintaining balance, flexibility, and long-term financial growth. The best strategy is not necessarily the most aggressive one. The best strategy is the one you can sustain consistently while continuing to strengthen your overall financial position.

Many homeowners begin with enthusiasm when trying to pay off debt early. They make large extra payments for several months, drastically cut spending, and temporarily become extremely disciplined. However, without a sustainable plan, burnout often follows. Unexpected expenses arise, motivation decreases, or lifestyle pressure becomes overwhelming. Eventually, many people abandon the strategy completely and return to minimum payments.

This chapter focuses on avoiding that cycle.

A successful mortgage acceleration plan must be realistic enough to survive real life. It should create progress without constantly creating stress. It should improve your financial future without destroying your present quality of life. Most importantly, it should adapt as your income, priorities, and opportunities evolve over time.

The first step in building a personalized strategy is understanding your mortgage itself. Many homeowners do not fully understand the structure of their loan. They know the monthly payment amount, but they may not know the interest rate, remaining balance, amortization schedule, or how much interest they will pay over time. Before creating an acceleration plan, you should analyze your mortgage carefully.

Understanding your loan gives you clarity. For example, homeowners with high interest rates may benefit significantly from refinancing if market conditions improve. Others with low fixed rates may decide to keep their current loan while focusing excess cash flow on investments or alternative financial goals. Some borrowers may have adjustable-rate mortgages that require additional planning due to future payment uncertainty. Every mortgage structure creates different strategic opportunities.

Once you understand the loan itself, the next step is evaluating your financial foundation. Accelerating mortgage payoff without proper financial stability can create unnecessary risk. Before aggressively directing large amounts toward principal reduction, homeowners should evaluate several important areas.

Emergency savings are critical.

Without adequate reserves, homeowners may become financially vulnerable during job loss, medical emergencies, unexpected repairs, or economic downturns. Many financial setbacks occur not because people lack income, but because they lack liquidity. A strong emergency fund protects progress and prevents homeowners from relying on high-interest debt during difficult periods.

Consumer debt should also be evaluated carefully. High-interest credit cards, personal loans, and other expensive debt obligations often reduce financial efficiency significantly.

In many situations, eliminating these obligations first improves monthly cash flow and creates stronger long-term mortgage acceleration potential.

Retirement planning also matters.

Some homeowners become so focused on paying off their mortgage that they neglect retirement contributions entirely. While debt reduction is important, long-term wealth creation usually requires balance. Compound growth inside retirement accounts can become extremely powerful over decades. A personalized mortgage strategy should consider both debt elimination and future investment growth.

Another important factor is income stability.

A homeowner with highly predictable income may feel comfortable implementing aggressive payoff strategies. Someone with fluctuating self-employment income or commission-based earnings may need greater flexibility and larger reserves. Financial plans should reflect the realities of income consistency and career stability.

Once your financial foundation is clear, you can begin designing the actual acceleration strategy.

One popular approach involves fixed monthly extra principal payments. This strategy is simple and highly effective over time. Even modest additional payments can shorten loan terms dramatically because they reduce future interest calculations. Consistency matters more than perfection. Small extra payments made regularly over many years can produce extraordinary results.

Another approach involves biweekly payment systems. Instead of making one monthly mortgage payment, homeowners divide the payment in half and pay every two weeks. Because there are twenty-six biweekly periods in a year, this strategy results in the equivalent of one extra full payment annually. Over time, this can reduce interest expense and accelerate payoff substantially.

Some homeowners prefer lump-sum reduction strategies. Instead of committing to large monthly extra payments, they apply bonuses, tax refunds, commissions, business profits, or investment gains toward principal reduction periodically throughout the year. This approach can provide flexibility while still accelerating progress significantly.

Cash-flow-based acceleration strategies are also becoming increasingly popular. These systems focus on improving monthly cash flow through budgeting, income growth, debt reduction, and strategic financial organization. Extra cash flow is then redirected toward mortgage elimination systematically.

There is no universal formula.

The most effective strategy often combines multiple methods together. For example, a homeowner may use biweekly payments while also applying annual bonuses toward principal reduction and directing rental income toward accelerated payoff. Combining systems creates momentum and flexibility simultaneously.

One important consideration when designing your strategy is motivation psychology.

Financial success is heavily influenced by behavior. If a plan feels too restrictive or overwhelming, consistency becomes difficult. Some homeowners benefit emotionally from seeing rapid progress through smaller milestone goals. Others prefer automated systems that reduce emotional decision-making altogether.

For example, one person may feel highly motivated by watching their mortgage balance decrease every month through extra payments. Another person may feel more motivated by increasing investment accounts simultaneously while gradually reducing debt. Understanding your personality helps create a strategy you are more likely to maintain long term.

Technology can greatly strengthen mortgage acceleration systems. Mortgage calculators, financial dashboards, automatic transfers, budgeting apps, and investment tracking tools create visibility and accountability. Automation is especially powerful because it reduces reliance on daily motivation and willpower.

Many financially successful individuals automate positive financial behavior entirely. Extra mortgage payments occur automatically after payday. Savings contributions happen automatically. Investment accounts receive scheduled deposits consistently. These systems transform discipline into habit.

Another critical aspect of personalized mortgage planning is flexibility during different life seasons.

Your financial priorities at age thirty may differ greatly from your priorities at age fifty-five. Young professionals may prioritize career growth and investment opportunities while still making moderate extra mortgage payments. Families with children may temporarily focus on stability and educational expenses. Individuals approaching retirement may shift aggressively toward debt elimination and income preservation.

Your strategy should evolve with you.

Rigid financial systems often fail because life changes

constantly. Income levels fluctuate. Opportunities appear unexpectedly. Economic conditions shift. Health situations evolve. The most successful financial plans allow adaptation while maintaining long-term direction. Risk tolerance also plays an important role.

Some homeowners experience tremendous emotional relief from aggressively eliminating debt. Others feel more comfortable maintaining low-interest mortgage debt while investing excess capital into businesses, real estate, or retirement accounts. Neither approach is automatically correct or incorrect. The key is making intentional decisions based on informed analysis rather than fear or emotion.

One of the greatest dangers in mortgage planning is comparison.

Many people compare themselves to friends, coworkers, or social media personalities who appear financially successful. This often creates pressure to make decisions that are misaligned with personal goals or circumstances. Financial freedom is highly personal. Your mortgage strategy should reflect your own priorities rather than external expectations.

Another major factor in long-term success is patience.

Mortgage acceleration is usually not an overnight

transformation. It is a process of gradual improvement, consistent action, and compound progress. Homeowners who remain disciplined through market cycles, economic uncertainty, and life transitions often achieve extraordinary financial outcomes over time.

Small improvements compound.

An extra payment here. A reduced expense there. A side income stream. A strategic refinance. A smart investment decision. Over years and decades, these actions combine into major financial transformation.

Perhaps most importantly, a personalized mortgage acceleration strategy creates empowerment. Instead of feeling trapped inside a thirty-year obligation, homeowners begin feeling proactive and intentional. Every payment becomes part of a larger plan. Every financial decision moves them closer toward freedom, stability, and flexibility.

This mindset shift is powerful.

People who once felt overwhelmed by debt often begin feeling optimistic because they can finally see progress and direction. Financial confidence grows as systems improve and momentum builds.

The goal is not simply paying off a mortgage.

The goal is creating a financial life built on control, flexibility, security, and opportunity. Mortgage acceleration becomes one component of a much larger wealth-building framework designed to support long-term freedom.

Your strategy does not need to look like anyone else's.

It simply needs to work for you consistently over time.

The homeowners who achieve lasting financial success are not always the highest earners or the most aggressive investors. Often, they are the people who understand themselves clearly, build intentional systems, stay disciplined during difficult periods, and continue moving forward steadily over many years.

A personalized mortgage acceleration strategy gives you that structure.

And once the structure is in place, financial freedom becomes not just a dream, but a measurable destination you move closer toward with every intentional decision you make.

The Teacher Who Built a Mortgage Freedom Plan One Step at a Time

When Rebecca Lawson bought her first home at thirty-six years old, she felt proud, grateful, and terrified all at the same time.

As a public school teacher, she never considered herself wealthy. Her income was stable but modest, and for years she believed homeownership might remain out of reach. After years of saving carefully, improving her credit, and working summer tutoring programs for extra income, she finally qualified for a mortgage on a small three-bedroom house in a quiet neighborhood.

The day she received the keys, she stood alone in the empty living room and smiled.

“This is mine,” she whispered quietly.

But within a few months, excitement slowly gave way to anxiety.

The mortgage payment felt enormous compared to her previous apartment rent. Property taxes surprised her. Maintenance expenses appeared unexpectedly. Every repair felt stressful because she no longer had a landlord to call.

One evening, after paying bills online, Rebecca stared at her mortgage statement and felt overwhelmed.

Thirty years.

The number haunted her.

She calculated how old she would be when the mortgage would finally be paid off if she continued making only minimum payments. The answer depressed her. She imagined decades of financial pressure stretching endlessly into the future. "I can't do this forever," she said quietly to herself.

Yet Rebecca also understood something important. She did not have the income to aggressively attack the mortgage the way some financial experts online recommended. She could not simply throw thousands of extra dollars toward the loan every month without risking financial instability.

For several weeks, she felt discouraged.

Then one Saturday morning while drinking coffee and reviewing her finances, she had a realization that changed everything.

She did not need to copy someone else's strategy.

She needed a strategy that fit her own life.

That single thought transformed her mindset.

Instead of feeling defeated because she could not follow extreme financial advice, Rebecca began building a personalized plan based on her actual income, goals, and lifestyle. She spent evenings researching mortgage acceleration techniques, budgeting systems, and long-term financial planning concepts.

The first thing she did was create clarity. She reviewed every expense carefully and discovered multiple areas where money quietly disappeared each month. Small online purchases, unused subscriptions, restaurant spending after stressful workdays, and convenience habits added up to far more than she realized.

Instead of making drastic cuts, she made gradual adjustments.

She canceled unnecessary subscriptions. She cooked at home more consistently. She redirected tutoring income toward savings and extra principal payments. Most importantly, she automated small additional mortgage payments every month.

At first, the extra amount was tiny.

Only one hundred dollars.

But when she entered the numbers into a mortgage payoff calculator, she was shocked by how much time and interest it could save over the life of the loan.

For the first time since buying the house, she felt hope.

The progress was slow initially, but emotionally powerful. Every month, she watched the principal balance decrease slightly faster than scheduled. Instead of feeling trapped by the mortgage, she began feeling in control of it.

That emotional shift changed her entire relationship with money. Rebecca also started focusing on income opportunities instead of only expense reduction. During summers, she expanded her tutoring business. Eventually, she created online educational study guides for students and teachers, selling them through digital platforms.

The extra income was inconsistent at first, but she remained disciplined.

Whenever additional money arrived, she followed a simple system. Part of it went toward emergency savings. Part went toward retirement investments. The rest went directly toward mortgage principal reduction.

Years earlier, she would have spent unexpected income impulsively because she viewed it as temporary bonus money.

Now, every dollar had a purpose connected to long-term freedom.

As time passed, Rebecca refined her strategy.

When interest rates dropped, she refinanced into a shorter loan term while maintaining manageable payments. She improved her budgeting systems without becoming obsessive. She increased retirement contributions gradually while still accelerating the mortgage.

Her strategy was not extreme.

It was sustainable.

That made all the difference.

Friends sometimes questioned why she focused so much on financial planning.

"You should enjoy life more," one coworker told her during lunch one afternoon.

Rebecca smiled politely.

What people did not understand was that financial organization had actually improved her quality of life dramatically. She slept better. She worried less constantly. She no longer felt panicked by every unexpected expense.

The mortgage was still there, but it no longer controlled her emotionally.

Ten years after buying the home, Rebecca sat on her back porch one quiet evening grading student assignments while watching the sunset. Her mortgage balance had decreased far faster than originally projected. Her emergency fund was fully established. Her retirement accounts were growing steadily. Most importantly, she finally felt financially stable.

For the first time in her life, she truly believed long-term freedom was possible.

One afternoon, a younger teacher named Melissa visited Rebecca after school looking discouraged.

"I don't think I'll ever get ahead financially," Melissa admitted. "I can barely imagine buying a house."

Rebecca recognized the fear immediately because she had once felt exactly the same way.

Instead of giving complicated financial advice, she shared one lesson that had changed her life.

"You don't need a perfect strategy," Rebecca said gently. "You need a strategy you can actually stick with."

Melissa listened carefully.

Rebecca explained how small consistent actions had transformed her financial life over time. Extra principal payments. Side income. Automated systems. Gradual lifestyle adjustments. Patience. Consistency.

Not perfection.

Years later, Rebecca would often reflect on how dramatically her mindset had changed since that first frightening year of homeownership. Back then, the mortgage felt like a life sentence. Now, it felt like a challenge she had learned to manage intelligently.

Eventually, the day arrived that once seemed impossibly distant.

Rebecca made her final mortgage payment.

The moment itself was quiet and surprisingly emotional. Sitting alone at her kitchen table, she stared at the confirmation screen on her laptop and felt tears fill her eyes.

Not because of the money.

Because of what the journey represented.

For years, she believed financial freedom belonged only to people with massive incomes, wealthy families, or extraordinary luck. But her experience taught her something far more powerful.

Financial freedom often belongs to ordinary people willing to create intentional systems, stay disciplined, and remain patient long enough for small actions to compound into extraordinary results.

Rebecca smiled quietly as she closed her laptop.

The house was finally hers.

But even more importantly, she had become someone who understood how to build lasting financial stability step by step, decision by decision, year by year. And that lesson would continue benefiting her long after the mortgage itself was gone.

Chapter 4

Using Income Growth to Accelerate Mortgage Freedom

One of the most powerful yet overlooked strategies for paying off a mortgage faster is increasing income intentionally. Many homeowners focus almost entirely on reducing expenses when trying to improve their financial position. While budgeting and controlling spending are extremely important, there is a limit to how much most people can realistically cut from their monthly expenses. Income growth, however, often has far greater long-term potential. When combined with intelligent financial systems, increased income can dramatically accelerate mortgage payoff while also improving quality of life, investment opportunities, and financial stability.

The relationship between income and mortgage freedom is not simply about earning more money. It is about learning how to direct additional income strategically instead of allowing it to disappear through lifestyle inflation. Many people experience income growth throughout their lives, yet they remain financially stressed because their expenses rise at the same pace as their earnings. Raises lead to larger car payments, more expensive vacations, luxury purchases, and higher monthly obligations. As a result, despite earning significantly more money over time, they never truly build financial freedom.

The key difference between financially trapped high earners and financially independent households often comes down to intentional income allocation.

When homeowners create systems that redirect portions of increased income toward debt reduction, investing, and wealth-building assets, financial acceleration begins to occur much faster. Mortgage payoff no longer depends solely on squeezing the existing household budget tighter every month. Instead, it becomes connected to growth, opportunity, and long-term strategic planning.

This chapter focuses on understanding how income growth can become one of the most effective tools for eliminating mortgage debt while simultaneously building a stronger financial future.

The first step is changing the way you think about income itself.

Most people view income as something fixed or controlled entirely by employers. They focus primarily on salaries and hourly wages. However, financially successful individuals often develop multiple income streams over time. They understand that relying entirely on one paycheck creates limitations and vulnerability. Additional income sources increase flexibility, strengthen cash flow, and create opportunities for faster financial progress.

Income growth can come from many different areas.

Career advancement is one obvious example. Improving skills, obtaining certifications, networking strategically, negotiating salaries, and pursuing leadership opportunities can increase earning potential substantially over time. Many homeowners underestimate how much their long-term income can grow if they intentionally invest in professional development.

For example, a person who increases annual income by even ten thousand dollars and strategically applies a significant portion toward mortgage reduction may eliminate years from their loan term. Over decades, career advancement combined with disciplined financial management can create extraordinary results.

However, employment income is only one possibility.

Side businesses have become increasingly common and accessible in the modern economy. Technology has created opportunities for people to generate income through consulting, freelancing, digital products, online education, e-commerce, content creation, coaching, and countless other services. Even modest side income can create major long-term financial acceleration when used intentionally.

One important psychological advantage of side income is that it often feels separate from normal household budgeting. Because the money was not previously relied upon for basic living expenses, homeowners may feel more comfortable directing it aggressively toward mortgage payoff or investing. This creates progress without feeling as restrictive as reducing lifestyle spending dramatically.

Rental income is another powerful mortgage acceleration tool.

House hacking, accessory dwelling units, short-term rentals, room rentals, and investment properties can generate cash flow that offsets housing expenses significantly. Some homeowners are able to eliminate large portions of their mortgage payment through rental strategies while simultaneously building equity and long-term real estate wealth.

This concept changes the way people think about homeownership entirely.

Instead of viewing a home purely as an expense, homeowners begin viewing real estate as a financial asset capable of producing income and supporting wealth creation. Over time, this shift in perspective can create powerful financial opportunities. Investment income also plays a role in long-term mortgage acceleration. Dividend-paying investments, business ownership, retirement account growth, and passive income streams may eventually contribute toward debt reduction or even replace employment income entirely. While building substantial investment income takes time, the long-term impact can be life-changing.

One of the most important principles in income-based mortgage acceleration is avoiding immediate lifestyle expansion.

Lifestyle inflation quietly destroys financial momentum for many households. Every time income rises, spending increases automatically. Larger homes, luxury vehicles, expensive dining, upgraded electronics, designer purchases, and recurring entertainment expenses become normalized quickly. Over time, higher income fails to create greater freedom because obligations rise equally fast.

Intentional homeowners interrupt this cycle.

Instead of spending every dollar of increased income, they create allocation systems. For example, someone may decide that every future raise will be divided strategically: part toward investing, part toward mortgage reduction, part toward savings, and part toward lifestyle improvement. This creates balance while still ensuring long-term progress.

The goal is not deprivation.

The goal is alignment between present enjoyment and future freedom.

Another powerful strategy involves directing irregular income toward mortgage acceleration. Bonuses, commissions, tax refunds, business profits, inheritance funds, royalty income, and investment gains can all become tools for principal reduction. Because these income sources are not always predictable monthly earnings, applying them toward debt reduction often feels psychologically easier than increasing fixed monthly obligations.

Some homeowners create annual mortgage reduction goals instead of focusing only on monthly progress. For example, they may commit to reducing the principal balance by an additional ten thousand dollars per year through bonuses, side income, and strategic cash-flow management. This flexible approach can create motivation while adapting to fluctuating income patterns.

Mindset also matters significantly when using income growth strategically.

Many people unconsciously increase spending to match social expectations as income rises. Expensive lifestyles become symbols of success. However, appearances can be deceptive. Some individuals with luxury lifestyles remain deeply trapped financially due to excessive debt and uncontrolled spending habits.

True financial freedom often comes from invisible discipline.

The homeowner quietly applying bonuses toward principal reduction may ultimately achieve far greater long-term security than the person constantly upgrading lifestyle expenses. Delayed gratification is one of the most powerful financial skills anyone can develop.

This does not mean avoiding enjoyment or success.

It means understanding the long-term trade-offs attached to financial decisions. Every dollar spent today carries an opportunity cost connected to future freedom, investment growth, or debt elimination.

Another important concept is scalability.

Some income strategies have limited growth potential, while others may expand dramatically over time. A small side business may eventually become a major income source. Rental properties may increase in cash flow and value over decades. Digital products may continue generating income long after the initial work is completed. Career expertise may lead to consulting opportunities or leadership roles. When homeowners begin viewing income growth as a long-term strategy rather than a short-term survival tool, their financial perspective changes dramatically.

Patience is essential during this process.

Income growth often develops gradually rather than instantly. Many successful businesses, investments, and careers require years of consistent effort before producing major financial rewards. The homeowners who benefit most from income acceleration strategies are often those willing to stay disciplined during the early stages when progress feels slow.

Consistency compounds.

An extra five hundred dollars per month directed toward principal reduction over many years can produce enormous savings. A growing side business generating increasing cash flow can eventually eliminate mortgage debt years earlier than expected. Investment income reinvested consistently can create long-term financial independence.

These results rarely happen overnight.

They happen through systems repeated consistently over long periods of time.

One major advantage of increasing income instead of relying entirely on expense reduction is emotional sustainability. Extreme budgeting often creates burnout because people feel deprived constantly. Income growth strategies, however, can create excitement, motivation, and optimism because they focus on expansion rather than restriction.

For many homeowners, the combination of moderate spending discipline and intentional income growth creates the ideal balance.

It allows them to enjoy life responsibly while still making aggressive financial progress.

Financial flexibility also improves dramatically when income rises strategically. Larger emergency reserves become possible. Investment opportunities become more accessible. Mortgage acceleration becomes easier. Retirement contributions increase. Stress decreases because homeowners feel less dependent on a single paycheck or financial outcome.

Perhaps most importantly, intentional income growth creates options.

Options are one of the greatest forms of financial power. The ability to reduce work hours, change careers, survive economic downturns, help family members, invest during opportunities, or retire earlier becomes possible when income systems and financial discipline work together.

Mortgage freedom is not only about eliminating debt.

It is about creating a life with greater flexibility, control, confidence, and opportunity.

Income growth accelerates that process because it expands the resources available to build the future you truly want.

The homeowners who achieve extraordinary financial progress are often not the people who simply earn the most money. They are the individuals who understand how to direct increased income intentionally instead of allowing it to disappear through unconscious spending habits.

Every raise, every side income stream, every investment gain, and every financial opportunity can become part of a larger system moving you closer toward freedom.

The key is creating intentional structures before the income arrives.

Because once income grows without a plan, lifestyle inflation often grows even faster.

This chapter is meant to help you recognize that increasing income is not merely about working harder endlessly. It is about building systems, opportunities, and financial habits that create long-term leverage. When income growth and mortgage acceleration work together strategically, the timeline toward financial freedom can shorten dramatically.

Your future is not determined only by what you earn today.

It is shaped by what you build, how you grow, and how intentionally you direct the opportunities that come into your life over time.

How Extra Income Can Cut Years Off a Mortgage

When Melissa first got the idea to start a small online consulting side business, she didn't think much of it beyond earning a little extra spending money. Around the same time, John was settling deeper into his career and expecting that their $400,000 mortgage would simply be a long-term part of life. At 6.5% interest and a monthly payment of about $2,528, it felt like a fixed reality they would slowly chip away at over 30 years.

But one evening, they sat down together and ran the full numbers on what "normal" actually meant. Over three decades, they would pay more than $910,080 in total, with over $510,000 of that going purely to interest. The number didn't just surprise them—it changed how they saw their entire financial situation. The mortgage stopped looking like a bill and started looking like a long-term wealth decision they could actively influence. That's when Melissa suggested something simple: instead of treating her new $1,000 monthly income as lifestyle money, what if they used it to attack the mortgage? At first, it didn't seem like a dramatic change. But when they applied it directly to principal, their effective payment jumped to $3,528 per month, and the projected payoff timeline dropped from 30 years to about 17.

As they committed to the plan, the results started compounding. That consistent $1,000 monthly contribution alone reduced their total interest from about $510,000 to roughly $320,000, saving nearly $190,000 over time. Then John received an annual bonus of about $5,000 after taxes. Instead of spending it, they applied it directly to the mortgage as well, adding another layer of acceleration.

Over time, those combined decisions reshaped everything. With both monthly and annual contributions working together, their mortgage timeline shrank further to about 14–15 years instead of 30. Total interest savings climbed past $250,000, and they realized they were on track to eliminate their mortgage during their strongest earning years rather than late in life when options would be more limited.

Eventually, the mortgage disappeared entirely—but their strategy didn't stop there. Instead of increasing spending, Melissa and John made a decision that would define their long-term future: they continued "paying themselves" by investing the same $3,528 per month into diversified investments averaging 8% returns. Over the next 15 years, that disciplined approach alone had the potential to grow into more than $1.2 million.

Looking back, what changed their trajectory wasn't just income—it was intention. Melissa's side business and John's bonuses didn't automatically create wealth. What created wealth was the decision to redirect that income instead of absorbing it into lifestyle. A standard 30-year mortgage became a much shorter financial path, followed by a long-term investment engine that built freedom, flexibility, and security far earlier than they ever expected.

One of the biggest financial debates homeowners face is whether they should aggressively pay off their mortgage early or invest their money for potentially higher long-term returns. Some financial experts argue that eliminating debt should always be the top priority because a paid-off home creates security, stability, and peace of mind. Others argue that low-interest mortgage debt can be strategically maintained while excess cash flow is invested into assets that may grow faster than the mortgage interest rate over time.

The truth is that both perspectives contain valid points.

The key is understanding that mortgage payoff and investing do not always need to compete against each other. In many situations, the most effective long-term financial strategy is a balanced approach that combines both debt reduction and wealth-building simultaneously.

This chapter focuses on how homeowners can strategically combine mortgage acceleration with investing to maximize long-term financial freedom, flexibility, and wealth creation.

Chapter 5

Combining Mortgage Payoff and Investing for Maximum Wealth

One of the biggest financial debates homeowners face is whether they should aggressively pay off their mortgage early or invest their money for potentially higher long-term returns. Some financial experts argue that eliminating debt should always be the top priority because a paid-off home creates security, stability, and peace of mind. Others argue that low-interest mortgage debt can be strategically maintained while excess cash flow is invested into assets that may grow faster than the mortgage interest rate over time.

The truth is that both perspectives contain valid points.

The key is understanding that mortgage payoff and investing do not always need to compete against each other. In many situations, the most effective long-term financial strategy is a balanced approach that combines both debt reduction and wealth-building simultaneously.

This chapter focuses on how homeowners can strategically combine mortgage acceleration with investing to maximize long-term financial freedom, flexibility, and wealth creation.

One of the first concepts homeowners must understand is opportunity cost.

Opportunity cost refers to the potential benefit lost when choosing one financial action over another. Every dollar used for mortgage payoff is a dollar that cannot simultaneously be invested elsewhere. Likewise, every dollar invested instead of paying down debt means the mortgage balance remains larger for longer.

This creates an important financial decision.

For example, if a homeowner has a mortgage interest rate of 4% but can potentially earn 8% long-term annual returns through diversified investments, mathematically the investments may outperform the interest savings over time. However, mathematics alone does not determine the best financial decision. Risk tolerance, emotional security, income stability, and life stage also matter significantly.

A paid-off home creates certainty.

Investments, while historically powerful over long periods, still involve volatility and uncertainty. Markets fluctuate. Businesses fail. Economic downturns occur. Mortgage payoff provides a guaranteed return equal to the interest rate being eliminated, while investments involve variable future performance.

This is why personal financial planning should never rely exclusively on mathematics alone.

Human behavior and emotional comfort matter too.

For some homeowners, aggressively paying off a mortgage provides tremendous emotional relief. The idea of eliminating monthly housing debt creates peace of mind that cannot easily be measured with spreadsheets. These individuals often sleep better knowing they own their home outright regardless of economic conditions.

For others, maintaining manageable low-interest mortgage debt while investing aggressively creates greater confidence because they see stronger long-term wealth-building opportunities through compound growth.

Neither approach is universally correct.

The best strategy often combines elements of both.

One balanced approach involves simultaneously making moderate extra mortgage payments while consistently investing for the future. This strategy allows homeowners to reduce debt faster than scheduled while still benefiting from long-term compound investment growth.

Compound growth is one of the most powerful forces in wealth creation.

When investments generate earnings that themselves begin producing additional earnings, long-term growth can accelerate dramatically. Time becomes extremely important because compounding works best over long periods. Even relatively modest consistent investments can grow substantially over decades.

This is why delaying all investing until after a mortgage is fully paid off may sometimes reduce long-term wealth-building potential.

For example, a homeowner who spends twenty years aggressively eliminating mortgage debt while completely neglecting retirement investing may miss valuable compound growth opportunities during their highest earning years.

Balance matters.

A strong financial plan usually considers both security and growth.

One effective strategy is creating percentage-based allocation systems. For example, a homeowner may decide that extra cash flow each month will be divided intentionally:

- Part toward extra mortgage principal
- Part toward retirement investing
- Part toward emergency savings
- Part toward taxable investments or income-producing assets

This creates financial diversification while still accelerating long-term progress.

Another important concept is liquidity.

Home equity can become substantial over time, but equity inside a home is relatively illiquid compared to cash or investment accounts. Accessing home equity often requires refinancing, selling the property, or obtaining loans against the property. Investments and cash reserves, however, may provide greater flexibility during emergencies or opportunities.

This is why some homeowners intentionally avoid putting every available dollar into mortgage payoff. Maintaining healthy liquidity can provide security and financial adaptability during unexpected situations.

Life changes constantly. Job loss, medical expenses, business opportunities, market downturns, and family emergencies can all create situations where liquidity becomes extremely valuable. A financially balanced homeowner may feel more stable knowing they have both growing equity and accessible investment reserves.

Interest rates also influence decision-making.

For homeowners with very low fixed mortgage rates, investing excess cash may appear more attractive mathematically because the borrowing cost is relatively inexpensive. For homeowners with higher mortgage interest rates, aggressive payoff may produce stronger guaranteed returns through interest savings.

Tax considerations may also play a role depending on individual circumstances, investment structures, and mortgage interest deductions. Financial planning should always consider the broader financial picture rather than focusing on one isolated metric.

Age and life stage are also critical factors.

Younger homeowners often benefit greatly from long-term compound investment growth because they have decades ahead for investments to mature. Older homeowners approaching retirement may prioritize debt elimination and income stability more heavily because reducing monthly obligations becomes increasingly valuable during retirement years.

This does not mean one strategy suddenly becomes wrong.

It simply means priorities evolve over time.

A young professional may focus heavily on investing while making moderate extra mortgage payments. A mid-career family may balance investing with accelerated debt reduction. Someone approaching retirement may aggressively eliminate remaining mortgage obligations while preserving investment accounts.

Flexibility is essential.

Financial plans should evolve as income, opportunities, responsibilities, and goals change throughout life.

Another powerful strategy involves investing first while planning future lump-sum mortgage reductions later. Some homeowners intentionally build investment accounts aggressively during high-growth years, then later use portions of investment gains or business sale proceeds to eliminate mortgage debt entirely.

Others prefer "hybrid acceleration," where mortgage payoff and investing occur simultaneously throughout the journey. This balanced approach often provides emotional stability because homeowners see progress in multiple areas at once. Behavioral psychology matters greatly here.

People are more likely to remain disciplined when they feel motivated and balanced rather than financially restricted. Seeing retirement accounts grow while also reducing mortgage balances can create powerful positive reinforcement.

One major mistake homeowners make is viewing mortgage payoff and investing as enemies.

In reality, both are tools.

The goal is not simply becoming debt-free or investment-rich individually. The goal is building a complete financial system that creates freedom, stability, flexibility, and long-term opportunity.

Wealth creation is rarely about maximizing one financial metric in isolation.

It is about optimizing your entire financial life strategically.

This includes protecting cash flow, reducing financial stress, building assets, preparing for retirement, maintaining flexibility, and creating long-term security for yourself and your family.

Another important factor is inflation.

Over long periods, inflation changes the value of money significantly. A fixed mortgage payment may become easier to manage over time as income rises and currency values change. Investments, businesses, and appreciating assets may also benefit from inflationary environments. Understanding how inflation interacts with debt and investing can influence long-term financial decisions.

At the same time, debt should never become an excuse for reckless leverage or poor financial discipline. Some homeowners become overly focused on maximizing investment returns while carrying excessive debt and inadequate reserves. True financial strength comes from balance and intentionality rather than excessive risk-taking.

Financial freedom is not created by gambling.

It is created by consistency, patience, discipline, and intelligent long-term decision-making.

One of the most important lessons in this chapter is recognizing that financial success is deeply personal. Some people value peace of mind above maximizing returns. Others prioritize aggressive wealth-building opportunities. Most homeowners benefit from a strategy somewhere between these extremes.

The best financial plan is not necessarily the one with the highest theoretical return on paper.

It is the plan you can follow consistently during both good times and difficult periods.

Consistency often matters more than optimization.

A homeowner consistently investing and moderately accelerating mortgage payoff for twenty years will usually achieve stronger results than someone constantly changing strategies emotionally based on headlines, fear, or market fluctuations.

Another critical lesson is that financial freedom is multidimensional.

A paid-off home alone does not automatically create wealth if there are no investments or income-producing assets. Likewise, large investment accounts may not feel emotionally satisfying if enormous debt obligations continue creating stress. The strongest financial positions often include both meaningful assets and reduced liabilities working together.

This creates balance, flexibility, and confidence.

The ultimate goal is creating a financial life where money supports your values, priorities, and long-term vision rather than controlling your decisions through stress and obligation.

Mortgage payoff and investing are not opposing forces. When combined intelligently, they can become powerful partners in building long-term wealth and financial independence.

The key is intentional planning.

Every dollar should move you closer toward a future defined not by financial pressure, but by opportunity, freedom, and lasting security.

Combining Mortgage Payoff and Investing at the Same Time

When David first started talking about paying down their mortgage faster, Sarah's reaction was simple—she just wanted something predictable. Their $500,000 home loan at 5.75% interest, with a monthly payment of about $2,917, already felt like a long-term commitment they had mentally accepted. But one weekend, they sat down and ran the full picture, and that's when things changed. Over 30 years, they would pay about $1,050,120 in total, including roughly $550,120 in interest alone. That number shifted the conversation completely—it wasn't just a mortgage anymore, it was a long-term financial decision shaping their entire future.

At first, David leaned toward going all-in on debt payoff. He wanted it gone as fast as possible. So they tested what that would actually look like: adding an extra $1,500 per month toward the mortgage and not investing anything else. Their new effective payment became $4,417 per month, and the payoff timeline dropped to about 14 years. On paper, it looked amazing—they would save roughly $310,000 in interest and eliminate their mortgage much earlier than expected. But Sarah noticed something important: during those same 14 years, they would be building zero investment growth.

That realization led them to step back and reconsider the trade-offs. Instead of choosing one extreme, they explored a more balanced approach. Rather than putting the full $1,500 toward the mortgage, they split it evenly—$750 toward extra principal and $750 into long-term investments earning about 8% annually. This adjusted their mortgage payment to around $3,667 per month and extended the payoff timeline to about 19 years instead of 14.

Even though the mortgage would take longer to disappear in this version, something more powerful started to emerge in the background. The interest savings were still meaningful—about

$190,000—but now they were also building a growing investment portfolio that reached approximately $420,000 during the same period. Instead of relying only on home equity, they were quietly building a second financial engine alongside it.

As time passed, the structure proved to be even more impactful than they initially expected. Once the mortgage was finally paid off, they didn't change their habits. Instead, they redirected the entire former payment of $3,667 per month into investments for another 10 years. At an 8% return, that second phase alone could grow to about $670,000, bringing their total investment assets to roughly $1,090,000 when combined with earlier growth.

Looking back, David and Sarah realized the biggest shift wasn't in the numbers—it was in how they framed the decision from the beginning. It was never just "pay off debt or invest." It was about structure. The aggressive approach created speed and certainty. The balanced approach created growth and diversification. And together, they showed something more important: the strongest financial outcomes often come from doing both at the same time, allowing debt reduction and wealth building to reinforce each other instead of competing.

[illegible]

One of the greatest misconceptions about financial freedom is the belief that success comes primarily from one perfect investment, one major business opportunity, or one dramatic financial breakthrough. While these opportunities can certainly accelerate wealth creation, the reality is that most long-term financial success is built through consistency rather than intensity. Mortgage freedom, investment growth, and lasting wealth are usually the result of disciplined habits repeated steadily over many years.

This chapter focuses on one of the most important yet underestimated aspects of financial success: long-term financial discipline.

Without discipline, even the best mortgage payoff strategies eventually fail. Budgets collapse. Investments stop. Extra payments disappear. Lifestyle inflation takes control. Emotional spending increases during stressful periods. Many homeowners begin their financial journey with enthusiasm and motivation but over time they lose consistency because they never developed sustainable systems and habits.

Chapter 6

Building Long-Term Financial Discipline and Staying Consistent

One of the greatest misconceptions about financial freedom is the belief that success comes primarily from one perfect investment, one major business opportunity, or one dramatic financial breakthrough. While large opportunities can certainly accelerate wealth creation, the reality is that most long-term financial success is built through consistency rather than intensity. Mortgage freedom, investment growth, and lasting wealth are usually the result of disciplined habits repeated steadily over many years.

This chapter focuses on one of the most important yet underestimated aspects of financial success: long-term financial discipline.

Without discipline, even the best mortgage payoff strategies eventually fail. Budgets collapse. Investments stop. Extra payments disappear. Lifestyle inflation takes control. Emotional spending increases during stressful periods. Many homeowners begin their financial journey with enthusiasm and motivation, but over time they lose consistency because they never developed sustainable systems and habits.

Discipline is what keeps progress moving forward when motivation fades.

Motivation is temporary. Discipline creates permanence.

One of the biggest challenges homeowners face is maintaining focus over long financial timelines. A mortgage often lasts decades. Investment growth compounds slowly during the early years. Debt reduction can initially feel frustrating because progress appears gradual. During these periods, many people become discouraged and abandon their plans before experiencing the powerful long-term effects of consistency.

Understanding the psychology of delayed gratification is essential.

Modern culture encourages immediate rewards. Advertising constantly promotes convenience, luxury, and instant satisfaction. Social media creates pressure to appear successful through visible spending. Expensive cars, vacations, restaurants, electronics, and luxury purchases are often presented as symbols of achievement. However, many people financing these lifestyles privately struggle with debt, stress, and financial insecurity.

Financial discipline often requires resisting short-term emotional impulses in favor of long-term freedom.

This does not mean avoiding enjoyment or living miserably. It means learning how to distinguish between temporary pleasure and lasting value. Every financial decision carries long-term consequences. Small repeated habits often shape financial futures far more than isolated major decisions.

For example, consistently directing extra funds toward mortgage principal reduction may not feel exciting in the moment. However, over many years, those small extra payments can save enormous amounts of interest and dramatically accelerate financial freedom. Likewise, consistent investing may seem slow initially, but compound growth eventually becomes extremely powerful.

The challenge is that compound progress is often invisible during the early stages.

Many people quit too soon because they expect immediate transformation.

This is why patience becomes one of the most valuable financial skills anyone can develop.

Long-term discipline begins with clarity of purpose. Homeowners who understand exactly why they want financial freedom tend to remain more consistent during difficult periods. Some people are motivated by reducing stress and anxiety. Others want retirement security, more family time, travel opportunities, or the ability to leave generational wealth behind. Some want freedom from dependence on employers or freedom to pursue meaningful work instead of simply chasing paychecks.

Purpose strengthens discipline.

When financial decisions connect to deeper personal goals, consistency becomes easier because progress feels emotionally meaningful rather than purely mathematical.

One effective strategy for maintaining discipline is visualization. Homeowners should regularly remind themselves what life could look like without mortgage debt. Imagine redirecting thousands of dollars each month toward investments, travel, charitable causes, family goals, or entrepreneurship. Imagine entering retirement without major housing expenses. Imagine the emotional peace of knowing your home is fully yours.

These mental images strengthen long-term commitment.

Another important aspect of discipline is creating systems that reduce emotional decision-making. Human beings are emotional creatures. Fear, stress, excitement, envy, and impulse often influence financial behavior more than logic.

This is why automation becomes extremely valuable.

Automatic mortgage overpayments, automated investment contributions, scheduled savings transfers, and recurring budgeting systems help remove emotional inconsistency from financial planning. Instead of relying on willpower constantly, disciplined systems operate automatically in the background.

For example, homeowners who automate extra principal payments immediately after payday are often far more consistent than those attempting to manually decide every month whether to send additional funds. Automation transforms good intentions into habitual action.

Tracking progress also strengthens discipline significantly.

Many people lose motivation because they fail to measure improvement. Watching mortgage balances decrease, investment accounts grow, and debts disappear creates positive reinforcement. Visible progress encourages continued consistency.

Some homeowners create milestone goals throughout their financial journey. Instead of focusing only on the distant goal of complete mortgage payoff, they celebrate smaller achievements along the way. Reaching the first fifty thousand dollars of equity, reducing the mortgage balance below a certain threshold, eliminating consumer debt, or achieving specific investment milestones can create powerful motivation.

Momentum matters psychologically.

Once progress becomes visible, people often feel increasingly motivated to continue.

Discipline also requires learning how to handle setbacks properly.

Financial journeys are rarely perfectly smooth. Unexpected expenses occur. Job loss, economic downturns, medical emergencies, family obligations, and market volatility can interrupt progress temporarily. Many people abandon their financial plans entirely after experiencing setbacks because they interpret temporary difficulties as failure.

Successful homeowners think differently.

They understand that setbacks are normal parts of long-term financial life. Instead of quitting, they adjust, recover, and continue moving forward. Flexibility combined with consistency is often more powerful than rigid perfection.

Emergency funds play a major role here.

Strong financial reserves protect discipline because they reduce the likelihood that unexpected expenses will destroy long-term plans. Homeowners without emergency savings often rely on credit cards or loans during crises, creating additional financial pressure that slows future progress.

Discipline also involves protecting yourself from comparison.

Social comparison destroys financial focus for many people. Watching friends, coworkers, or influencers display luxury lifestyles can create pressure to spend emotionally rather than strategically. However, appearances are often misleading. Many people living expensive lifestyles privately struggle with enormous debt and financial insecurity.

True financial discipline sometimes requires being comfortable looking less wealthy temporarily while quietly building long-term freedom.

The person driving a modest car while aggressively investing and reducing debt may ultimately achieve far greater security than the individual constantly upgrading appearances through borrowing.

Another important principle is identity.

Long-term financial success often occurs when disciplined behavior becomes part of personal identity rather than temporary effort. Instead of saying, "I'm trying to save money," financially disciplined individuals begin viewing themselves as people who manage money intentionally. Instead of seeing investing or mortgage acceleration as occasional tasks, they become integrated lifestyle habits.

Identity-driven behavior tends to last longer because it aligns actions with self-image.

For example, someone who sees themselves as financially responsible will naturally make decisions consistent with that identity even when external motivation decreases.

Environment also matters greatly.

The people surrounding you influence financial behavior significantly. Constant exposure to impulsive spending culture, negative attitudes, or financially reckless environments can weaken discipline over time. Conversely, surrounding yourself with financially intentional individuals often strengthens long-term consistency.

Education plays a continuing role as well.

Financial discipline grows stronger when homeowners continue learning about investing, debt management, wealth creation, taxes, cash flow, and long-term planning. Education increases confidence and helps people make informed decisions instead of reacting emotionally to headlines or market fluctuations. Another critical lesson is that discipline compounds similarly to investments.

Small disciplined actions repeated daily create massive long-term effects. Spending slightly less than you earn consistently. Investing every month consistently. Applying extra principal consistently. Avoiding unnecessary debt consistently. Improving income gradually. Over decades, these behaviors create extraordinary transformation.

The opposite is also true.

Small undisciplined habits repeated consistently can quietly destroy long-term financial progress. Excessive lifestyle inflation, emotional spending, neglected savings, and unmanaged debt gradually compound negatively over time.

Financial discipline is ultimately about alignment.

It means aligning daily actions with long-term goals rather than temporary emotions. It means making intentional choices repeatedly even when results are not immediately visible. It means understanding that wealth is often built quietly, steadily, and patiently over long periods.

One of the greatest rewards of discipline is confidence.

As homeowners remain consistent over time, fear gradually decreases. Financial systems strengthen. Cash reserves grow.

Debt shrinks. Investments expand. Stability increases. Eventually, people begin realizing they are no longer trapped financially. They have options.

That transformation is powerful.

Financial freedom is not simply about numbers on a spreadsheet. It is about reduced stress, greater flexibility, stronger relationships, and the ability to make life decisions without constant financial pressure.

Discipline creates that freedom slowly but reliably.

The homeowners who ultimately achieve extraordinary financial outcomes are often not the smartest investors, the highest earners, or the luckiest individuals.

They are frequently the people who simply stayed consistent longer than everyone else.

Consistency creates momentum.

Momentum creates confidence.

Confidence creates freedom.

And over time, those small disciplined decisions repeated year after year become the foundation of a completely different financial life.

How Small Consistent Actions Create Massive Long-Term Results

At first, David and Sarah weren't thinking in terms of strategies or financial models at all—they were just looking at their monthly mortgage statement and wondering why so much of their long-term income seemed tied up in interest. But as they dug deeper into the numbers on their $500,000 home loan, they began to see something different. The mortgage wasn't just a bill—it was a system. And depending on how they used their extra cash flow, it could either slow them down for decades or become the foundation for accelerating their entire financial future.

With a $500,000 mortgage at 5.75% interest and a monthly payment of about $2,917, they quickly realized the long-term cost of doing nothing beyond the minimum. Over 30 years, they would pay about $1,050,120 in total, including roughly $550,120 in interest alone. That realization changed the way they viewed every extra dollar—they were no longer just "extra payments," but potential leverage for either debt freedom or wealth building.

They first tested a pure acceleration approach. In this version, they added $1,500 per month directly to the mortgage and did not invest anything extra elsewhere. This increased their effective payment to $4,417 per month and shortened their mortgage timeline to about 14 years. The outcome was powerful: they would save roughly $310,000 in interest and eliminate their mortgage far earlier than expected. But they also noticed a trade-off—during those same 14 years, all surplus capital was locked into the home, with no parallel investment growth.

Next, they explored a more balanced approach. Instead of putting the entire $1,500 toward debt, they split it evenly: $750 toward the mortgage and $750 into investments growing at an estimated 8% per year. This adjusted their mortgage payment to about $3,667 per month and extended the payoff timeline to about 19 years instead of 14.

While the mortgage was paid off more slowly in this version, something important began to happen in the background. The mortgage still lost nearly $190,000 in interest over time, but now they were also building an investment portfolio that grew to approximately $420,000 during the same period. Instead of choosing between debt reduction and investing, they were doing both at once.

After the mortgage was finally eliminated, the strategy shifted again. They redirected the full former payment of $3,667 per month into investments for another 10 years. At an 8% return, this second phase alone could grow to about $670,000, bringing their total investment portfolio to roughly $1,090,000 when combined with earlier contributions.

In the end, the lesson became clear. The decision wasn't really about paying off a mortgage or investing—it was about structure. One path delivered faster certainty and lower interest, while the other built long-term diversification and compounding wealth. The strongest outcomes came from understanding that financial progress is not an either-or decision, but a system designed over time to reduce debt while simultaneously building assets.

Chapter 7

Creating Your Lifetime Financial Freedom Plan

Paying off a mortgage early is an extraordinary accomplishment, but true financial freedom extends beyond the elimination of one debt. A paid-off home can dramatically improve cash flow, reduce stress, and create stability, yet homeowners who achieve lasting financial independence understand something even more important: mortgage freedom should become the foundation of a much larger long-term wealth strategy.

This chapter focuses on building a complete lifetime financial freedom plan.

Many people spend years working toward mortgage payoff but fail to prepare for what comes afterward. Once the mortgage disappears, they suddenly have significant extra cash flow available every month. Without a structured plan, that money can easily disappear through lifestyle inflation, impulsive spending, or financial drift. However, when homeowners intentionally redirect former mortgage payments toward investing, income-producing assets, and long-term planning, financial acceleration can become extraordinary.

The elimination of mortgage debt is not the finish line.

It is the beginning of a new financial stage where flexibility, wealth creation, and opportunity expand dramatically.

One of the most powerful concepts in long-term financial planning is understanding the role of fixed expenses in shaping freedom. For decades, many households organize their lives around recurring obligations. Mortgage payments, car payments, credit card debt, student loans, and other liabilities consume large portions of monthly income. As these obligations disappear, financial breathing room increases significantly.

This increase in flexibility changes everything.

A homeowner without a mortgage often requires far less income to maintain the same lifestyle. This creates options. Some people choose to work less. Others invest more aggressively. Some pursue entrepreneurship, travel, charitable projects, or early retirement. Others continue building wealth rapidly because their monthly obligations have decreased dramatically.

Financial freedom is ultimately about options.

The more flexibility you create financially, the more control you gain over your time, decisions, career choices, and future opportunities. However, true financial freedom requires more than simply eliminating debt. It requires intentional planning for the decades ahead. Many homeowners underestimate future financial needs such as healthcare costs, inflation, retirement income requirements, long-term care, family support, and economic uncertainty. A complete financial freedom plan addresses these realities proactively instead of reactively.

The first major component of a lifetime plan is cash-flow management after debt elimination.

When the mortgage is finally paid off, homeowners should avoid the temptation to immediately absorb the freed-up cash flow into lifestyle expansion. This is one of the biggest financial mistakes people make after reaching major financial milestones. Larger homes, expensive vehicles, luxury spending, and unnecessary obligations can quickly recreate financial pressure.

Instead, intentional homeowners redirect cash flow strategically.

For example, someone who previously paid $3,000 monthly toward a mortgage could redirect that same amount into investments, retirement accounts, business opportunities, or income-producing assets. Over time, the wealth-building potential becomes enormous because the individual is already psychologically accustomed to living without that money available for discretionary spending.

This creates powerful financial leverage.

One important principle in long-term planning is that income-producing assets eventually become more valuable than earned income alone. Employment income depends on continued labor. Investments, businesses, rental properties, royalties, dividends, and other assets can continue generating income even when a person reduces work hours or retires entirely.

This transition from earned income dependency to asset-generated income is a major milestone in financial freedom.

Mortgage elimination often accelerates this transition because the absence of housing debt frees up substantial monthly resources for investment growth.

Retirement planning also becomes significantly easier once major debts disappear. Many people approaching retirement feel stressed because they still carry large mortgage balances and monthly obligations. Eliminating debt before retirement can dramatically reduce the amount of retirement income required to maintain financial stability.

For example, a household requiring $8,000 monthly while carrying a mortgage may only require $4,500 or $5,000 monthly once the home is fully paid off. This difference can greatly reduce retirement pressure and improve long-term security.

Inflation must also be considered carefully.

Over time, living costs generally rise. Healthcare, insurance, food, taxes, and services may become significantly more expensive over decades. A lifetime financial freedom plan should include investments and income strategies designed to outpace inflation rather than simply preserving cash.

This is why long-term investing remains extremely important even after debt elimination.

Some homeowners mistakenly believe financial planning ends once the mortgage disappears. In reality, the post-mortgage years often represent the most important wealth-building phase because large amounts of cash flow become available for strategic growth.

Diversification is another essential concept.

Relying entirely on one income source, one investment, or one asset class creates vulnerability. Strong financial freedom plans often include multiple layers of protection and opportunity. Retirement accounts, brokerage investments, real estate, business income, cash reserves, insurance planning, and estate planning all work together to create stability and resilience. Emergency planning remains important as well.

Even financially successful households experience unexpected situations. Economic downturns, health issues, family emergencies, lawsuits, market volatility, or unexpected repairs can occur at any stage of life. Maintaining strong reserves and flexible financial structures helps preserve freedom during difficult periods.

Another major component of long-term planning is protecting lifestyle flexibility.

Many people spend decades sacrificing their health, relationships, and happiness chasing financial success, only to discover they never learned how to enjoy the freedom they worked so hard to create. A balanced financial life includes not only wealth accumulation, but also intentional living.

Money should support your values rather than replace them.

Some homeowners use financial freedom to spend more time with family. Others travel, mentor younger generations, support charitable causes, or pursue meaningful personal projects. The purpose of financial independence is not merely accumulating numbers inside accounts. It is creating the ability to live intentionally without constant financial pressure controlling decisions.

Estate planning also becomes increasingly important over time.

Homeowners who build substantial equity, investments, and assets should consider how wealth will transfer to future generations or charitable causes. Wills, trusts, beneficiary designations, insurance planning, and tax strategies all play roles in preserving long-term financial security for families.

Generational wealth is often created through intentional planning rather than sudden wealth alone.

Teaching financial principles to children and future generations can become one of the greatest long-term gifts homeowners provide. The habits of discipline, investing, strategic thinking, and intentional money management often create far greater lasting impact than money itself.

Mindset remains critically important throughout the journey.

Many people believe financial freedom will instantly eliminate all stress or problems. While reduced debt certainly improves stability, financial independence is ultimately more about peace, flexibility, and control than perfection. Emotional discipline, gratitude, and intentionality remain important regardless of net worth.

Comparison should also be avoided.

True financial freedom looks different for every person. Some people value simplicity and low stress. Others enjoy entrepreneurship, investing aggressively, or building large portfolios. The key is aligning your financial life with your personal priorities rather than external expectations or social pressure.

Technology and automation can continue strengthening long-term financial systems as well. Automated investing, financial tracking systems, estate planning tools, and tax optimization strategies all help preserve consistency and organization over decades.

Another important lesson is that freedom grows gradually.

Most financially independent individuals did not experience overnight transformation. Instead, they built systems steadily over many years. Small extra payments became mortgage freedom. Mortgage freedom became investment growth. Investment growth became flexibility. Flexibility became long-term independence.

Compound progress changes lives.

The process may feel slow initially, but eventually momentum becomes extraordinary. A homeowner who consistently invests former mortgage payments for twenty years after debt elimination may build substantial wealth even without massive income increases. Patience remains essential throughout the journey.

Financial freedom is not a race against other people. It is a long-term process of creating stability, flexibility, and intentionality step by step.

One of the most beautiful aspects of financial independence is the reduction of fear. As debts decrease, reserves increase, and assets grow, people often begin feeling calmer and more confident about the future. Decisions become less reactive and more intentional. Opportunities become easier to pursue because survival pressure decreases.

This emotional transformation is one of the greatest rewards of disciplined financial planning.

The ultimate goal of a lifetime financial freedom plan is not simply becoming wealthy.

It is creating a life where money becomes a tool rather than a source of constant stress and limitation.

A paid-off home is powerful.

But a paid-off home combined with strong investments, multiple income streams, financial discipline, long-term planning, and intentional living can create something even greater:

Lasting freedom.

The decisions you make today shape not only your mortgage timeline, but also the quality, flexibility, and opportunities available throughout the rest of your life.

Every extra payment, every disciplined habit, every investment contribution, and every intentional financial decision compounds into a future that becomes increasingly stable, flexible, and empowered over time.

Financial freedom is not one moment.

It is a system built carefully over years that eventually allows you to live with greater peace, confidence, and control over your future.

How a Paid-Off Mortgage Can Lead to Million-Dollar Wealth Growth

When Robert and Angela bought their home, they saw it the same way most homeowners do at first—a milestone, a place to settle, and a long-term monthly payment that would quietly follow them for decades. Their mortgage was $450,000 at 5.5% interest, with a standard payment of about $2,555 per month. It felt manageable, even normal. But one evening, while reviewing their long-term financial projections, they realized something that changed their perspective completely.

If they simply followed the 30-year schedule, they would end up paying nearly $919,800 in total, including about $469,800 in interest alone. That meant almost half a million dollars would go to interest instead of building their own wealth. That realization became the turning point. Instead of asking, "How do we just pay this off eventually?" they started asking, "What if we controlled how fast this disappears—and what happens after it does?"

Robert suggested an aggressive approach. They decided to add an extra $1,200 per month directly toward the mortgage principal. This increased their total monthly payment to $3,755 and immediately changed the structure of the loan. What had once been a 30-year commitment now began shrinking rapidly. With consistent payments, their mortgage timeline dropped to about 16 years instead of 30, saving them roughly 14 years of payments.

As they stayed consistent, the impact became undeniable. Over time, this strategy reduced their total interest paid to about $255,000 instead of nearly $470,000. That meant they saved approximately $215,000 simply by redirecting money with intention. But what made the strategy even more powerful was what came next—what they did after the mortgage disappeared. When the mortgage was finally paid off, Robert and Angela didn't change their lifestyle. Instead, they made a deliberate decision to continue living as if the mortgage still existed—but now they would pay themselves. They redirected the full $3,755 per month into long-term investments averaging about 8% annual returns. Over the next 14 years, that consistent discipline could grow into more than $1.4 million.

Then they added another layer. Throughout the entire process, they also contributed an additional $1,000 per month into retirement accounts. Over 30 years, assuming similar long-term growth, this alone could grow to around $1.5 million. Together, these two investment streams create a combined portfolio of approximately $2.9 million.

By the end of the journey, the outcome was completely different from what they originally expected. They had a fully paid-off home, nearly $3 million in investments, and the ability to generate approximately $116,000 per year in retirement income at a conservative 4% withdrawal rate—about $9,666 per month—without a mortgage payment.

Looking back, Robert and Angela realized the most important shift wasn't just paying off debt faster. It was what they did after. The mortgage wasn't just eliminated—it was transformed into a long-term wealth-building engine. By accelerating payoff and then redirecting that same cash flow into investments, they created a system that turned a fixed obligation into decades of financial freedom, stability, and generational wealth potential.

Chapter 8

The Final Mortgage Freedom Blueprint

Reaching financial freedom is rarely the result of one single strategy. It is usually the outcome of many intelligent financial decisions working together consistently over time. Mortgage payoff, investing, income growth, cash-flow management, discipline, and long-term planning all combine to create a complete financial system capable of transforming a person's future. This final chapter brings all of those principles together into one comprehensive mortgage freedom blueprint designed to help homeowners create lasting financial independence.

Throughout this series, you have explored many different mortgage payoff strategies. You learned how small payment adjustments can shorten loan terms dramatically. You explored refinancing strategies, lump-sum reductions, rental income opportunities, investing alongside debt reduction, and income acceleration systems. You also learned that financial freedom is not only about eliminating debt, but about building flexibility, stability, confidence, and long-term wealth.

The purpose of this chapter is to unify those lessons into a practical long-term framework. One of the biggest mistakes people make in personal finance is focusing too heavily on isolated tactics while ignoring the larger system. For example, someone may aggressively pay down mortgage debt while neglecting retirement savings entirely. Another person may focus exclusively on investing while ignoring dangerous consumer debt and poor cash flow management. Others constantly chase financial trends without developing consistency or discipline.

The strongest financial plans are integrated.

Every part of the financial system should support the larger goal of freedom.

This begins with understanding that your mortgage is not simply a monthly bill. It is one component of your entire financial ecosystem. The way you manage your mortgage affects cash flow, investment opportunities, retirement planning, emotional stress, career flexibility, and long-term wealth creation.

The first part of the final blueprint is financial awareness.

Many homeowners spend years reacting to finances instead of intentionally directing them. They pay bills automatically without analyzing where their money is going or whether their financial decisions align with long-term goals. Financial freedom begins when awareness replaces avoidance.

Awareness means understanding your mortgage balance, interest rate, amortization schedule, monthly obligations, net worth, income streams, investment accounts, and spending patterns clearly. You cannot optimize a financial system you do not fully understand.

Clarity creates control.

Once homeowners gain awareness, the next step is strengthening financial foundations. Before aggressively accelerating mortgage payoff, a strong foundation should include:

- Emergency reserves
- Controlled consumer debt
- Organized cash flow
- Consistent budgeting systems
- Basic retirement contributions
- Stable insurance protection

Without a solid foundation, aggressive financial strategies may create instability during difficult periods. The goal is sustainable progress rather than temporary intensity. Cash flow becomes the engine powering the entire blueprint.

A household with strong cash flow gains flexibility, opportunity, and resilience. Improved cash flow allows homeowners to make extra principal payments, invest consistently, build reserves, and handle unexpected expenses more comfortably. This is why managing spending, increasing income, and avoiding unnecessary debt remain critical throughout every stage of the journey.

Income growth also plays a central role in the blueprint.

Many people underestimate how much additional income can transform their long-term financial future. Career advancement, business ownership, side income, consulting, rental properties, digital products, and investments can all accelerate mortgage payoff dramatically when managed intentionally.

The key is directing income growth strategically instead of allowing lifestyle inflation to consume it automatically.

Lifestyle inflation quietly delays financial freedom for millions of people. As income rises, expenses expand equally fast. Larger homes, luxury vehicles, expensive habits, and recurring obligations create the illusion of success while often increasing long-term financial pressure.

Intentional homeowners interrupt this cycle.

They allow some lifestyle improvement while still prioritizing future freedom. Every raise, bonus, or side income opportunity becomes partially directed toward debt reduction, investing, and long-term wealth creation.

Another critical part of the blueprint is automation.

Human beings are emotional. Motivation fluctuates. Life becomes busy. Financial discipline weakens during stressful periods. Automated systems reduce the risk of inconsistency.

Automatic mortgage overpayments, investment contributions, savings transfers, and budgeting systems help create reliable long-term progress even during periods of low motivation. Automation transforms discipline into habit.

Consistency matters more than perfection.

This principle appears repeatedly throughout successful financial journeys. Small actions repeated consistently often outperform extreme short-term efforts followed by burnout. A homeowner consistently applying moderate extra principal payments for twenty years may achieve greater results than someone attempting unsustainable aggressive strategies temporarily.

Patience becomes extremely important.

Financial freedom compounds gradually. Mortgage balances decrease slowly at first. Investment growth feels small during early years. Income systems take time to mature. Many people quit too early because they expect rapid visible transformation.

Compound progress rewards those who remain disciplined long enough.

Over time, momentum becomes extraordinary. Debt shrinks faster. Investment growth accelerates. Cash flow improves. Stress decreases. Opportunities expand.

One of the most powerful phases of the blueprint occurs after major debt elimination.

When homeowners finally eliminate large mortgage obligations, enormous financial leverage becomes available. Thousands of dollars previously directed toward debt payments can now flow toward investments, businesses, travel, charitable causes, family support, or lifestyle flexibility.

This transition is life-changing.

However, homeowners must remain intentional during this stage. Without a plan, freed-up cash flow may disappear into unconscious lifestyle expansion. The blueprint requires strategic redirection of money toward long-term goals even after debt elimination.

Investing remains critically important throughout the entire process.

Mortgage payoff creates stability and guaranteed interest savings, while investing creates long-term growth and inflation protection. The most effective financial systems usually combine both. Homeowners who balance debt reduction with consistent investing often achieve stronger long-term flexibility and wealth than those focusing exclusively on one area.

Diversification also strengthens long-term security.

Relying entirely on one employer, one investment type, or one income source increases vulnerability. A resilient financial plan may include retirement accounts, brokerage investments, real estate, business ownership, emergency reserves, and multiple income streams working together.

The blueprint also recognizes the emotional side of money.

Financial stress affects relationships, sleep, health, confidence, and decision-making. A homeowner overwhelmed by debt often feels trapped emotionally. As financial systems improve, emotional freedom often improves as well.

Confidence grows when:

- Cash reserves increase
- Debt decreases
- Investments grow
- Income becomes diversified
- Long-term plans become clearer

Eventually, people begin realizing they no longer fear the future the way they once did.

This emotional transformation is one of the greatest rewards of financial discipline.

The blueprint also emphasizes flexibility over rigidity.

Life changes constantly. Economic conditions shift. Careers evolve. Families grow. Opportunities appear unexpectedly. Financial plans should adapt while maintaining long-term direction. Successful homeowners adjust strategies intelligently instead of abandoning goals during temporary setbacks.

Another essential principle is intentional living.

Money is not the ultimate goal.

Freedom is.

The purpose of mortgage acceleration, investing, and financial planning is not merely accumulating wealth endlessly. It is creating the ability to live according to your values without constant financial pressure controlling every decision.

For some people, that means early retirement. For others, it means entrepreneurship, travel, helping family members, charitable work, or simply living with peace of mind.

The blueprint should support the life you truly want.

Comparison must also be avoided.

Every homeowner's journey is different. Income levels, family responsibilities, risk tolerance, career paths, and personal priorities vary significantly. Financial success should be measured by alignment with personal goals rather than external appearances.

Many wealthy-looking individuals privately struggle with debt and financial stress. Meanwhile, financially disciplined households quietly build substantial long-term wealth without needing to display it publicly.

True financial freedom is often invisible.

Another important lesson in the blueprint is that wealth creation becomes easier as obligations decrease. Every debt eliminated increases flexibility. Every investment contribution strengthens future stability. Every disciplined habit compounds positively over time.

Eventually, momentum begins working for you instead of against you.

The homeowner who once felt trapped by debt may eventually experience a completely different reality:

- A paid-off home
- Growing investments
- Multiple income streams
- Reduced stress
- Career flexibility
- Retirement security
- Financial confidence

That transformation rarely occurs overnight.

It is built slowly through intentional systems repeated consistently over many years.

The final blueprint is ultimately simple in concept, though powerful in execution:

- Strengthen financial foundations
- Improve cash flow
- Increase income intentionally
- Reduce unnecessary debt
- Automate positive financial behavior
- Invest consistently
- Accelerate mortgage payoff strategically
- Avoid destructive lifestyle inflation
- Stay disciplined long term
- Redirect freed-up cash flow toward future wealth

These principles working together create extraordinary long-term results.

Financial freedom is not reserved for the lucky or the wealthy.

It is often achieved by ordinary people willing to remain disciplined, intentional, and patient long enough for compound progress to transform their lives.

Every extra payment matters.

Every investment contribution matters.

Every disciplined decision matters.

Over time, those decisions compound into something far greater than money alone:

Peace.

Confidence.

Flexibility.

Opportunity.

Freedom.

And that is the true purpose of the ultimate mortgage payoff game plan.

Combining Multiple Strategies Into One Complete Mortgage Freedom Plan

When Mark and Jennifer first bought their home, it felt like the beginning of a long but predictable chapter. Their mortgage was $600,000 at 6% interest, with a monthly payment of about $3,598. Like most homeowners, they assumed they would simply pay it down slowly over 30 years and eventually own it outright later in life.

But one night, while reviewing their long-term financial outlook, they ran the full numbers. Over 30 years, they would end up paying about $1,295,280 in total, including roughly $695,280 in interest alone. That realization hit differently than they expected. Nearly $700,000 would go to interest—money that would never come back to them. That moment shifted the conversation from "how do we manage this mortgage" to "how do we control its timeline and redirect everything we save afterward?"

Mark was the first to act. He proposed an aggressive but structured plan: add $1,000 per month directly toward the mortgage principal. Jennifer agreed, but only if they stayed consistent and intentional. With that decision, their monthly payment increased to $4,598, and the mortgage timeline immediately began to shrink. Instead of 30 years, they were now on track for roughly 18 years, saving about $305,000 in interest just from that one adjustment.

As they committed to the plan, they added another layer. Mark's job began producing annual bonuses averaging $10,000 after taxes, and instead of spending them, they applied every dollar directly toward the mortgage. Combined with their monthly overpayments, they were now accelerating principal by about $22,000 per year. This pushed their payoff timeline even further down to around 14–15 years and increased total interest savings to more than $415,000. At the same time, Jennifer insisted they not focus only on debt. They began investing $1,500 per month into retirement and brokerage accounts earning an estimated 8% return. While the mortgage was shrinking faster than expected, their investment account was quietly growing in the background. Over 15 years, this alone could grow to approximately $520,000—creating a second major financial foundation alongside their home.

Then came the turning point of the entire strategy. Once the mortgage was fully paid off, they didn't allow lifestyle inflation to absorb the freed-up cash flow. Instead, they redirected the full $4,598 monthly payment into investments. For the next 15 years, this disciplined reinvestment phase had the potential to grow to approximately $1.6 million on its own.

When they combined everything—the earlier investment account and the post-mortgage investing phase—the result became something far larger than they initially imagined. Together, their strategy could produce approximately $2.12 million in investments, along with a fully paid-off home and over $415,000 in mortgage interest savings.

By the end of the journey, their financial picture had completely changed. If their investments generated a conservative 4% withdrawal rate, they could potentially create about $84,800 per year in retirement income—around $7,066 per month—without any mortgage payment at all. Looking back, Mark and Jennifer realized the breakthrough wasn't any single tactic. It was the combination of all of them working together: extra principal payments, disciplined use of bonuses, consistent investing, and the decision to redirect cash flow after debt elimination instead of increasing spending. The mortgage didn't just disappear—it became the starting point for a long-term wealth system that created freedom, flexibility, and financial confidence for decades to come.

Chapter 9

Avoiding the Biggest Financial Mistakes That Delay Mortgage Freedom

Building financial freedom is not only about making good decisions. It is also about avoiding the costly mistakes that quietly destroy momentum over time. Many homeowners work hard, earn good incomes, and genuinely want to improve their financial future, yet they remain trapped financially for decades because repeated mistakes continuously delay progress. Some of these mistakes are obvious, while others are subtle habits that slowly weaken long-term wealth creation year after year.

This chapter focuses on identifying and avoiding the most common financial mistakes that prevent homeowners from reaching mortgage freedom and long-term financial independence.

One of the biggest mistakes people make is living without a clear financial plan.

Many homeowners drift financially for years. They make monthly payments, react to expenses, and occasionally save money, but they never create a structured strategy for debt reduction, investing, income growth, or long-term wealth creation. Without direction, financial decisions become reactive instead of intentional.

A mortgage payoff plan should never exist only in your imagination.

It should be measurable, organized, and connected to specific goals. Homeowners who create written plans with timelines, payment targets, investment goals, and financial systems tend to make far greater progress because clarity improves discipline and decision-making.

Another major mistake is ignoring cash flow.

Many people focus heavily on income while neglecting spending habits and financial efficiency. A high income alone does not guarantee wealth. Countless high earners remain trapped in debt because uncontrolled spending absorbs every dollar they make. Lifestyle inflation becomes especially dangerous as income rises.

Lifestyle inflation occurs when expenses automatically expand alongside earnings. Larger homes, luxury vehicles, expensive vacations, dining habits, subscriptions, and recurring obligations quietly increase monthly financial pressure. Instead of using increased income to accelerate freedom, people unintentionally trap themselves in larger financial commitments.

This cycle can continue indefinitely.

A person earning twice as much income may still feel financially stressed if expenses expanded equally fast. True financial progress occurs when income grows faster than lifestyle obligations.

Another costly mistake is carrying high-interest consumer debt while neglecting repayment strategy.

Credit card debt is particularly destructive because high interest rates consume enormous amounts of cash flow over time. Many homeowners attempt to accelerate mortgage payoff while simultaneously carrying expensive revolving debt. In many cases, prioritizing high-interest debt elimination first creates stronger long-term financial efficiency.

For example, aggressively prepaying a mortgage at 5% interest while carrying credit card balances at 22% interest often slows overall financial progress dramatically. Strategic prioritization matters.

Emotional spending is another hidden financial destroyer.

Many people use spending as a coping mechanism for stress, boredom, frustration, loneliness, or social pressure. Online shopping, impulse purchases, luxury upgrades, and convenience spending often provide temporary emotional satisfaction while quietly weakening long-term financial stability.

The danger is not necessarily one large purchase.

The danger is repeated emotional behavior becoming normalized.

Financial freedom requires awareness of spending psychology. Homeowners must learn how to distinguish between intentional purchases aligned with values and emotional purchases driven by temporary feelings.

Another major mistake is failing to prepare for emergencies.

Unexpected expenses are inevitable. Job loss, medical bills, vehicle repairs, home maintenance issues, economic downturns, and family emergencies occur throughout life. Homeowners without emergency reserves often rely on credit cards, loans, or retirement withdrawals during crises, creating long-term financial setbacks.

Emergency funds protect momentum.

Without reserves, even disciplined homeowners may experience major disruptions to mortgage payoff plans and investment growth during difficult periods. Building financial security requires planning for uncertainty rather than assuming life will always remain stable.

Many people also underestimate the importance of insurance protection.

Health insurance, disability coverage, life insurance, homeowners insurance, and liability protection all play critical roles in long-term financial stability. One major uninsured event can destroy years of financial progress extremely quickly.

Ignoring retirement planning is another dangerous mistake.

Some homeowners become so focused on eliminating mortgage debt that they neglect retirement investing entirely during their highest earning years. While mortgage acceleration is valuable, retirement accounts benefit enormously from compound growth over long periods of time.

Time matters greatly in investing.

A person who delays retirement contributions for ten or fifteen years may lose substantial long-term growth potential that becomes difficult to recover later. Financial balance is essential. Debt reduction and investing should often work together rather than compete against each other.

Another common mistake is constantly changing financial strategies based on emotions or headlines.

Many homeowners become reactive during economic uncertainty. They panic during market downturns, stop investing when fear increases, or abandon long-term plans because of temporary economic conditions. Others chase financial trends, constantly switching investment strategies or debt reduction methods without remaining consistent long enough for results to compound.

Consistency matters more than excitement.

Wealth is usually built through disciplined long-term systems rather than constant emotional reactions to short-term events.

Comparison is another major financial trap.

Social media and modern culture constantly encourage comparison with others. Luxury lifestyles, expensive homes, vacations, vehicles, and visible consumption create pressure to spend beyond sustainable levels. However, appearances are often deceptive. Many people displaying wealth publicly are privately burdened by enormous debt and financial stress.

True financial strength is often quiet.

The homeowner driving a modest car while aggressively investing and reducing debt may ultimately achieve far greater freedom than the person financing appearances through endless borrowing.

Another dangerous mistake is relying entirely on one income source.

Economic conditions change. Industries evolve. Companies restructure. Job security is never guaranteed permanently. Homeowners depending completely on one paycheck often experience greater financial vulnerability and stress.

Multiple income streams create resilience.

Side businesses, investments, rental income, consulting, digital products, and passive income systems increase stability and flexibility significantly over time. Additional income also accelerates mortgage payoff and investing opportunities dramatically.

Some homeowners also make the mistake of viewing their home only as a personal expense instead of part of a larger financial system.

Real estate can create equity growth, rental opportunities, tax advantages, refinancing flexibility, and wealth-building potential when managed strategically. Understanding how to use real estate intelligently is an important component of long-term financial planning.

Another major issue is failing to track progress. What gets measured improves.

Homeowners who regularly review mortgage balances, investment growth, cash flow, spending patterns, and financial goals tend to remain more disciplined and motivated. Without visibility, it becomes easy to drift financially and lose focus.

Financial avoidance creates long-term damage.

Many people avoid reviewing statements, calculating debt totals, or analyzing spending because it creates discomfort. However, clarity is empowering. Understanding your financial reality honestly allows you to improve it intentionally.

Tax inefficiency is another overlooked issue.

Many homeowners fail to take advantage of retirement accounts, investment tax strategies, business deductions, or long-term planning opportunities that could improve financial efficiency substantially over time. Professional financial and tax guidance can sometimes produce significant long-term benefits.

Another mistake is underestimating the power of time.

Small financial decisions compound enormously over decades. A few hundred dollars invested monthly, moderate extra mortgage payments, controlled spending habits, and consistent discipline may seem insignificant short term, but over long periods they create extraordinary transformation.

The opposite is also true.

Small negative habits repeated consistently can quietly destroy wealth-building momentum. Minor overspending, neglected investing, unnecessary debt, and lifestyle inflation may appear harmless individually but compound negatively over years.

Patience is essential.

Many homeowners become discouraged because progress feels slow initially. Mortgage balances decrease gradually at first. Investments grow slowly during early years. Side businesses take time to develop. However, compound progress eventually accelerates dramatically for those who remain disciplined long enough.

One of the greatest financial mistakes people make is quitting too early.

The homeowners who achieve lasting financial freedom are often not the most talented or highest earning individuals. They are frequently the people who simply stayed consistent longer than others.

Another important lesson is that perfection is unnecessary.

Some people become paralyzed because they fear making mistakes or believe they must follow perfect financial strategies. In reality, progress matters far more than perfection. Small consistent improvements usually outperform occasional extreme efforts.

Flexibility also matters.

Financial plans should evolve with changing life stages, opportunities, responsibilities, and economic conditions. The goal is not rigid perfection. The goal is maintaining long-term direction while adapting intelligently over time.

Ultimately, avoiding financial mistakes is about intentionality.

Every financial decision either strengthens or weakens future freedom. Every dollar spent, invested, borrowed, or saved influences long-term outcomes. The more intentional homeowners become, the stronger their financial systems grow.

Mortgage freedom is not usually destroyed by one catastrophic mistake.

More often, it is delayed by repeated small behaviors that slowly weaken momentum over many years.

The good news is that small positive behaviors work the same way in reverse.

Consistent investing.

Controlled spending.

Extra mortgage payments.

Income growth.

Emergency reserves.

Long-term discipline.

Over time, these habits compound into extraordinary financial transformation.

The homeowners who recognize and avoid the biggest financial mistakes place themselves in a far stronger position to build not only a paid-off home, but also lasting wealth, flexibility, and peace of mind for the future.

How Financial Mistakes Can Cost Hundreds of Thousands of Dollars

When Chris and Amanda bought their home, it felt like they were stepping into a stable, predictable version of adulthood. The mortgage was $550,000 at 6.25% interest, with a monthly payment of about $3,386. At first, it didn't feel overwhelming—just another long-term responsibility they would manage alongside life, career growth, and family expenses. But over time, something subtle started to change. As Chris's income increased and Amanda's career stabilized, their lifestyle began to expand without much planning. A newer car payment showed up at $1,100 per month, dining out became more frequent at an additional $700, and vacations slowly grew to about $500 more per month than before. Individually, each decision felt small. Together, they created a financial structure that quietly pushed them further away from building wealth.

At the same time, credit card balances began to accumulate. A $25,000 revolving balance at 21% interest didn't feel urgent at first, but over time it became a silent drain. Even if they only made minimum payments, they could end up repaying around $50,000 or more—meaning over $25,000 would go directly to interest. Meanwhile, the mortgage remained untouched beyond minimum payments, and investing took a back seat to everyday spending.

After 30 years, the outcome of this path becomes clear. The mortgage is finally paid off, but very little wealth was built along the way. A large portion of their income was absorbed by interest payments and lifestyle inflation, leaving them with limited retirement savings and years of financial stress that felt unavoidable in hindsight.

Then there is the alternative version of their story.

In this version, Chris and Amanda make a very different set of decisions early on. Instead of allowing lifestyle inflation to absorb every raise, they intentionally direct $1,000 per month toward extra mortgage principal and commit $1,200 per month toward long-term investing. They also make a firm rule: no credit card balances carried month to month, and all raises and bonuses are assigned a purpose before they are spent.

With that structure in place, their financial trajectory begins to change quickly. Their mortgage payment increases to $4,386 per month, and the payoff timeline drops from 30 years to about 18 years. Over time, this disciplined approach saves them approximately $289,000 in interest, reducing total interest paid from about $669,000 to roughly $380,000.

At the same time, their investing does not wait for the mortgage to disappear. By consistently investing $1,200 per month at an estimated 8% return over 30 years, they build an investment portfolio worth approximately $1.8 million. Instead of having all their financial energy tied up in a single asset, they begin building wealth in parallel.

Once the mortgage is finally eliminated around year 18, the strategy shifts again. Now they redirect the full $4,386 monthly payment into investments for the remaining 12 years. This second phase alone can grow to approximately $1.1 million, simply from continuing the same disciplined cash flow they were already used to paying. When both phases are combined, the outcome is dramatically different. They end up with roughly $2.9 million in investments, a fully paid-off home, and significantly reduced financial stress throughout the journey. More importantly, they avoid high-interest debt, eliminate major financial pressure earlier in life, and gain long-term flexibility they never would have reached under a lifestyle-inflated approach.

The key lesson in Chris and Amanda's story is not about income—it's about direction. Both scenarios started with the same mortgage and similar opportunities. The difference came from behavior repeated over time. One path allowed spending to grow unchecked, while the other assigned every dollar a role. Over decades, that difference turned into hundreds of thousands of dollars in interest savings and millions in wealth accumulation.

Chapter 10

The Ultimate Mortgage Payoff Game Plan in Action

At this point in the series, you have explored a wide range of strategies: accelerating payments, leveraging income growth, avoiding financial mistakes, balancing investing with debt reduction, and building disciplined long-term habits. The final step is bringing everything together into one cohesive, real-world system. This is where theory becomes execution. This is where scattered financial ideas become a structured, repeatable, and scalable plan for long-term financial freedom.

The ultimate mortgage payoff game plan is not a single strategy. It is a layered system that adapts to your income, lifestyle, goals, and stage of life while consistently moving you toward one destination: financial independence.

Most homeowners fail not because they lack information, but because they lack integration. They may understand refinancing, extra payments, investing, or side income individually, but they never combine them into a unified system. As a result, progress is inconsistent. Some months are strong, others are weak, and over time, motivation fades. The purpose of this final chapter is to show how all the pieces fit together.

The ultimate game plan has four core pillars:

1. Cash flow optimization
2. Income expansion
3. Strategic debt acceleration
4. Long-term wealth building

When these four systems work together, financial progress becomes exponential instead of linear.

Cash flow optimization is the foundation.

Without control over cash flow, no strategy can be sustained long term. Homeowners must understand exactly where their money is going every month. This includes fixed expenses, variable expenses, debt obligations, and discretionary spending. Once clarity is established, money can be redirected intentionally.

The goal is not extreme restriction.

The goal is elimination of waste and alignment of spending with long-term priorities. Even small leaks in cash flow can dramatically slow mortgage payoff. Subscriptions, impulse purchases, unused services, and lifestyle inflation can quietly absorb thousands of dollars per year. Redirecting even a portion of this wasted cash flow toward mortgage principal or investments can significantly accelerate financial progress.

The second pillar is income expansion.

Income determines the ceiling of financial potential. While budgeting and expense control are important, they are inherently limited. There is only so much spending that can be reduced before quality of life is affected. Income growth, however, has virtually unlimited upside over time.

The ultimate game plan encourages homeowners to build at least one additional income stream. This could be a side business, consulting work, freelance income, rental property cash flow, or digital product revenue. The key is not the method itself, but the consistency of applying that income toward financial acceleration instead of lifestyle inflation.

Every additional dollar earned becomes a strategic tool.

Some dollars reduce debt. Some build investments. Some strengthen emergency reserves. Some improve quality of life intentionally. The key is direction, not randomness.

The third pillar is strategic debt acceleration. Not all debt is managed equally. High-interest consumer debt must often be eliminated aggressively before optimizing mortgage payoff. Mortgage debt, however, can be strategically accelerated using a combination of extra payments, lump-sum contributions, refinancing strategies, and income allocation.

The most effective mortgage acceleration systems are flexible.

They adapt to income changes, interest rates, and financial opportunities. Some months may allow for larger payments. Others may require minimal contributions due to temporary financial constraints. The system must remain consistent without becoming rigid.

A common mistake is trying to accelerate the mortgage too aggressively without maintaining financial stability. This creates burnout, stress, and eventual abandonment of the strategy. The ultimate game plan avoids this by balancing aggression with sustainability.

The fourth pillar is long-term wealth building.

Paying off a mortgage is only one part of financial freedom. True independence comes from assets that generate income over time. These may include retirement accounts, brokerage investments, real estate, business ownership, or other income-producing assets. The most powerful strategy is often combining mortgage acceleration with consistent investing.

This creates a dual-track system: one path eliminates debt while the other builds long-term wealth simultaneously.

Many homeowners mistakenly believe they must choose between paying off a mortgage or investing. In reality, the strongest financial outcomes often come from doing both in a structured, intentional way.

Once these four pillars are combined, the system begins to function as a whole.

Cash flow improvements provide extra money. Income growth expands financial capacity. Strategic debt reduction eliminates obligations faster. Investments build long-term wealth. Together, they create compounding financial momentum.

One of the most important aspects of the ultimate game plan is sequencing.

Financial priorities must be ordered correctly. For example, building emergency savings often comes before aggressive mortgage acceleration. Eliminating high-interest debt often comes before investing heavily. Increasing income may take priority during certain life stages.

The system is not static.

It evolves. Another critical factor is time horizon.

Short-term thinking often leads to poor financial decisions. Long-term thinking allows homeowners to make strategic sacrifices today for greater freedom tomorrow. The ultimate game plan always prioritizes long-term results over short-term comfort.

Discipline is the engine behind execution.

Without discipline, even the best strategy fails. With discipline, even a simple strategy can produce extraordinary results over time. Discipline ensures that extra payments are made consistently, investments continue regardless of market conditions, and income opportunities are pursued steadily.

However, discipline does not mean perfection.

The ultimate game plan allows for flexibility. Life will always include unexpected expenses, emotional moments, opportunities, and challenges. The goal is not to eliminate variability, but to maintain direction through it.

One of the most powerful outcomes of this system is psychological transformation.

Homeowners who follow a structured financial plan begin to feel more in control of their future. Anxiety decreases. Confidence increases. Financial decisions become intentional rather than reactive. Instead of feeling trapped by money, they begin to feel empowered by it.

This psychological shift is just as important as the financial results.

As the system compounds over time, progress accelerates. Mortgage balances shrink faster. Investments grow larger. Income streams strengthen. Cash reserves increase. Financial pressure decreases.

Eventually, the homeowner reaches a point where financial decisions are no longer driven by survival, but by choice.

That is the true definition of financial freedom.

It is not just having more money. It is having options.

Options to work less. Options to invest more. Options to travel. Options to support family. Options to take risks. Options to live according to personal values instead of financial constraints.

The ultimate mortgage payoff game plan is not a short-term tactic.

It is a lifelong framework.

It adapts to every stage of life while consistently pushing toward one outcome: increasing financial independence over time. When applied consistently, even moderate income households can achieve extraordinary results. The combination of discipline, structure, and long-term thinking often outweighs income level alone.

Financial freedom is not reserved for the highest earners.

It is available to anyone willing to build and follow a system.

This chapter represents the full integration of everything in this series. It is the transition point between learning strategies and executing them as a complete financial system.

From this point forward, success depends not on knowledge alone, but on consistent action over time.

The Complete Integrated Mortgage Payoff System in Action

When Thomas first brought up the idea of paying off the mortgage faster, it was during a late evening conversation with Laura at the kitchen table. They weren't in financial distress—their life was stable, their income was strong—but the $650,000 mortgage at 6.5% interest with a $4,112 monthly payment still felt like a long shadow over their long-term plans. Over 30 years, they would end up paying about $1,480,320 in total, including more than $830,000 in interest alone. That number stuck with them more than anything else. Laura was the first to suggest that maybe the problem wasn't just the mortgage—it was how they were using their cash flow. They went line by line through their monthly spending and found about $600 in expenses they no longer really valued or needed. Around the same time, Laura decided to start a small consulting side business, which began generating an extra $1,800 per month. Suddenly, they weren't just cutting costs—they were creating an additional $2,400 per month in controllable cash flow.

Instead of choosing one direction, Thomas proposed something more structured. They split the $2,400 evenly: $1,200 toward extra mortgage payments and $1,200 toward long-term investing. This immediately changed their mortgage structure. Their new effective payment became $5,312 per month, and the payoff timeline dropped from 30 years to about 17 years. What had once felt like a lifetime commitment was now being cut almost in half.

As they stayed consistent, the financial impact became undeniable. Over time, this strategy reduced their total mortgage interest from about $830,320 to roughly $450,000, saving around $380,320 simply through disciplined cash flow allocation. But at the same time, they were also building wealth in parallel. By investing $1,200 per month for 17 years at an average 8% return, they grew an investment portfolio to approximately $360,000 while still paying down their home aggressively. When the mortgage was finally eliminated in year 17, their strategy entered its most powerful phase. Instead of increasing lifestyle spending, they redirected the full $5,312 monthly payment into investments for another 13 years. That consistent reinvestment alone had the potential to grow to about $1.3 million, simply by continuing the same discipline they had already built.

When both phases were combined, the result was far greater than they initially expected. Their first investment phase and post-mortgage investment phase together created approximately $1.66 million in total investments, alongside a fully paid-off home. They also gained over $380,000 in interest savings, multiple income streams, and a level of financial flexibility they had never experienced before.

Looking back, Thomas and Laura realized the transformation didn't come from one big decision. It came from alignment. Every part of their financial life—spending, income, debt reduction, and investing—was working together instead of competing. That's what turned a standard 30-year mortgage into a structured 17-year payoff and a long-term wealth engine that continued growing well after the debt was gone.

Final Tips and Suggestions for Mortgage Freedom

Turning Strategy Into Lifelong Financial Independence

Achieving mortgage freedom is not simply about reaching a day where a loan balance finally hits zero. It is about a much deeper transformation—one that changes how a person thinks about money, stability, time, and opportunity. At the beginning of most homeowners' journeys, the mortgage feels like a fixed obligation, something that must be carried for decades without much flexibility. But over time, as income grows and financial awareness expands, the mindset shifts. The real question is no longer "How do I just get rid of this debt?" but instead becomes "How do I use this debt strategically while building something greater alongside it?" This shift marks the beginning of financial maturity. It is the moment where a mortgage stops being viewed only as a burden and starts being seen as a tool within a larger financial system that can either limit progress or accelerate it depending on how it is managed.

Most people never reach this stage of thinking because they stay focused only on making payments and hoping time takes care of the rest. But financially successful homeowners begin to realize that time alone is not a strategy. Time without structure simply extends outcomes. Time combined with intentional systems, however, can completely reshape a financial future. This is where the real power begins—not in how much money is earned, but in how that money is directed. A mortgage is not just a monthly bill; it is a long-term interest structure that quietly determines how much wealth is lost over decades. Once this is understood clearly, every financial decision begins to look different. Extra payments, investment decisions, savings habits, and even lifestyle choices all start to carry long-term consequences that either speed up or slow down financial freedom.

One of the most important realizations in this journey is that motivation is not enough to create lasting financial change. Many homeowners start strong when they first decide to pay down debt or invest more aggressively. They feel motivated, inspired, and disciplined for a few months or even a year. But life inevitably becomes busy again. Expenses appear. Priorities shift. Unexpected situations arise. And slowly, the original financial plan weakens. This is why systems are far more powerful than motivation. A system is something that continues to function even when motivation disappears. Automatic transfers to principal, scheduled investments, structured budgeting rules, and predefined cash flow allocations remove emotional decision-making from the equation. Instead of asking, “Should I make an extra payment this month?" the system already makes that decision in advance. This is what separates short-term effort from long-term transformation.

As financial awareness grows, another powerful principle emerges: paying yourself first in the correct direction. Most people misunderstand this concept. They believe it means saving whatever is left after spending. But in reality, it means intentionally directing money toward your future before lifestyle expansion consumes it. When income increases, the default human behavior is to improve lifestyle—better cars, nicer vacations, upgraded homes, and increased discretionary spending. While there is nothing wrong with enjoying life, unchecked lifestyle inflation quietly destroys long-term wealth potential. Instead, when a structured approach is used, every increase in income is divided with purpose. A portion goes toward debt reduction, a portion goes toward investing, a portion strengthens savings, and only then does lifestyle improvement take place. This ensures that every financial gain improves both present life and future security at the same time.

Another critical layer in this journey is the protection and management of cash flow. Income alone does not determine financial success. Many high-income individuals still feel financially stressed because their cash flow is poorly structured. Cash flow is what remains after obligations are met, and it determines how much flexibility a person truly has in life. Without healthy cash flow, even strong income becomes unstable. Unexpected expenses create stress. Job changes become risky. Investment opportunities are missed. Strong financial systems always prioritize cash flow stability first. This includes maintaining emergency reserves, avoiding high-interest debt, and ensuring that monthly obligations do not exceed sustainable income levels. When cash flow is strong, financial decisions become easier, more flexible, and far less emotional.

A major hidden force in long-term mortgage decisions is interest. Interest is often overlooked because it is spread out over time, making it feel small in the short term. However, over 20 to 30 years, it becomes one of the largest wealth transfers in a household's financial life. Every mortgage payment contains both principal reduction and interest cost, and the interest portion represents money that does not return to the homeowner. This is why extra principal payments have such a powerful effect. They do not just reduce debt—they eliminate future interest that would have been paid over decades. This creates a compounding benefit in reverse: every dollar applied early saves multiple dollars in the future. Once this concept is fully understood, financial behavior naturally begins to shift toward earlier and more intentional debt reduction. At a higher level, long-term financial success is not about choosing between debt payoff and investing—it is about combining both in a structured way. Many people mistakenly believe they must choose one path. Either they aggressively pay off their mortgage or they invest heavily. But the most effective financial systems often integrate both simultaneously. Debt reduction creates stability and reduces financial pressure, while investing builds long-term growth and opportunity. When both are happening at the same time, wealth begins to grow from multiple directions. Debt decreases, investments increase, and financial flexibility expands. Over time, this dual approach produces a much stronger and more resilient financial foundation than any single strategy alone.

Eventually, the mortgage itself becomes less of a central focus and more of a milestone within a larger plan. The real transformation happens not at the moment of payoff, but in what comes after. Once the mortgage is eliminated, a significant amount of monthly cash flow is suddenly freed. For many homeowners, this is the largest financial shift of their lives. Without preparation, this moment can lead to lifestyle inflation, where spending simply expands to absorb the newly available money. But with proper planning, this moment becomes the beginning of financial acceleration. The same money that once went toward debt can now be redirected into investments, income-producing assets, savings, or retirement planning. This is where wealth begins to grow exponentially instead of linearly. True financial freedom is not created through a single decision or a single strategy. It is built through years of consistent behavior, structured systems, and intentional financial direction. It requires patience, discipline, and the ability to delay gratification in exchange for long-term stability. It is not about being perfect with money, but about being consistent with direction. Small decisions repeated over time—extra payments, consistent investing, controlled spending, and disciplined cash flow management—create outcomes that feel almost exponential when viewed years later.

Ultimately, mortgage freedom is not the end goal. It is the starting point of a larger financial evolution. It represents the moment where financial pressure begins to decrease and financial opportunity begins to expand. When homeowners commit to building systems instead of relying on motivation, directing income instead of reacting to it, and balancing debt reduction with wealth building, their mortgage becomes more than a liability. It becomes the foundation of a long-term wealth strategy that can support financial independence, lifestyle flexibility, and generational opportunity for decades to come.

planning. This is where wealth begins to grow exponentially instead of linearly. True financial freedom is not created through a single decision or a single strategy. It is built through years of consistent behavior, structured systems, and intentional financial direction. It requires patience, discipline, and the ability to delay gratification in exchange for long-term stability. It is not about being perfect with money, but about being consistent with direction. Small decisions repeated over time—extra payments, consistent investing, controlled spending, and disciplined cash flow management—create outcomes that feel almost exponential when viewed years later.

Ultimately, mortgage freedom is not the end goal. It is the starting point of a larger financial evolution. It represents the moment where financial pressure begins to decrease and financial opportunity begins to expand. When homeowners commit to building systems instead of relying on motivation, directing income instead of reacting to it, and balancing debt reduction with wealth building, the mortgage becomes more than a liability. It becomes the foundation of a long-term wealth strategy that can support financial independence, lifestyle flexibility, and generational opportunity for decades to come.

www.ingramcontent.com/pod-product-compliance
Lightning Source LLC
LaVergne TN
LVHW040519210926
848480LV00007BA/1519
9798256009502